The Villa Rossa Series

Intercultural Perspectives on Italy and Europe

Volume II
Series Editor: Barbara Deimling

UNDER THE DEVIL'S SPELL
WITCHES, SORCERERS, AND THE INQUISITION
IN RENAISSANCE ITALY

MATTEO DUNI

SUF

Published for
Syracuse University in Florence
Florence, Italy
www.syr.fi.it

Book design: Brenda Cooke
Printed by Tipografia La Marina, Italy
ISBN 88-95250-01-1

Distributed by
Syracuse University Press
Syracuse, New York 13244-5160
www.SyracuseUniversityPress.syr.edu

CONTENTS

UNDER THE DEVIL'S SPELL
WITCHES, SORCERERS, AND THE INQUISITION
IN RENAISSANCE ITALY

CHAPTER I
THE FOUNDATIONS OF THE WITCH-HUNT

CHAPTER II
THE PRACTICE OF MAGIC: AN ITALIAN CITY
DURING THE RENAISSANCE

APPENDIX
INQUISITION TRIALS AGAINST SORCERESSES AND MAGICIANS

FOREWORD

From the fifteenth century to the eighteenth, witch-hunting engulfed Europe. It was believed that witches flew to Black Sabbats, signed pacts with Satan, and worked evil magic to undermine Christian society. Tens of thousands of people, mostly women, were tried, often tortured, and many died at the stake for the crime of diabolical witchcraft and demonic possession.

Under the Devil's Spell: Witches, Sorcerers, and the Inquisition in Renaissance Italy, by SUF Professor Matteo Duni, transports us into the midst of this drama, making the tragic stories of those involved tangible through the translated trial records. We hear about Don Guglielmo Campana, the fearsome wizard-priest, the enchantress Anastasia, and the country healer Brighento Brighenti.

The book is yet another of Professor Duni's research initiatives at Syracuse University in Florence (SUF). In Fall 2006, SUF hosted an international conference on witches in trials and treatises from the fourteenth century to the seventeenth, in collaboration with the University of Florence. Nineteen leading scholars from Europe, Israel and the United States convened to discuss new findings, and to present new approaches in the field of witchcraft studies. Professor Duni also teaches a course on witchcraft each semester at SUF.

It is therefore a particular pleasure to announce the publication of *Under the Devil's Spell*, as the second volume highlighting the academic work of SUF faculty and professional staff in *The Villa Rossa Series: Intercultural Perspectives on Italy and Europe*.

Barbara Deimling
Director
Syracuse University in Florence

Preface

WE LIVE IN AN AGE OF CULTURE WARS—ONE IN WHICH COMPETING systems for explaining the world and for guiding social behavior clash in both utterly profound and shockingly banal ways. In this study of witchcraft and sorcery, Matteo Duni places us in the midst of an earlier culture war, one that raged across Europe for much of the early modern period, occupying the attention of authorities both religious and secular, generating thousands of books, treatises, and trial records, and claiming tens of thousands of victims. To some contemporaries—especially those in positions of high authority in Church and state—it was a war between God and the devil, between the forces of good and evil. Their opponents, or so they believed, were those who had been deceived into entering into a pact with Satan; and the victims were those who had become the objects of the magic and sorcery that Satan's allies practiced. The "witches" and "sorcerers" (as well as their clients) had a different opinion, of course. Indeed it is unlikely that they gave much thought to what larger meanings their activities signified, since they were not seeking grand designs but rather very practical remedies to the kinds of problems that have occupied most human beings throughout history: the illness of a child, the threat of drought, the finding and binding of a lover. The methods they employed in order to have some control over their fate—the starving of roosters, the casting of beans, the collecting of dew on the night of Saint John the Baptist—were valued for their efficacy. What mattered was that the remedies worked.

Duni surveys this clash of cultures as it was played out in northern Italy from the late fourteenth through the late sixteenth centuries, paying particular attention to the city of Modena in the Po River valley. This world of Renaissance Italian magic and witchcraft is likely to be new to most English-speaking readers who are probably more familiar with the witch crazes that occurred in Protestant northern Europe and in Puritan New England. Given the circulation of books like Heinrich Krämer's *Malleus Maleficarum* throughout Europe, Italian witch-hunting shared many characteristics with its northern European counterpart;

but it also exhibited some distinctive features. For one thing, the prosecution of magic and witchcraft in Italy followed its own trajectory. During much of the fifteenth century lay authorities took the lead in the prosecution of witches; and in the late fifteenth and early sixteenth centuries several witch crazes occurred, especially in the Alpine regions. Then in the middle decades of the sixteenth century the inquisitors' focus shifted to the eradication of Protestantism on the Italian peninsula. Following the Council of Trent, the uprooting of "superstition" became the inquisitors' primary concern; but the Roman Church's increasingly skeptical attitude regarding the reality of the witches' sabbat prevented the kind of mass prosecutions that were then taking place across northern Europe.

Given the inquisitors' success in keeping Italy within the Catholic fold, another distinctive feature of Italian witchcraft was the frequent deployment by "witches" of objects, rituals, and words borrowed from Catholic liturgy. This is understandable since the Church itself claimed to be able to tap into a world of supernatural powers, powers which, if they fell into the wrong hands, could be used for maleficent purposes. More startling still, at least to modern eyes, was the frequent involvement of the Catholic clergy in magical practices as "wizard-priests." One in particular—Don Guglielmo Campana, parish priest and exorcist of the cathedral of Modena—figures prominently in this book and has been the subject of a separate study by Duni (Matteo Duni, *Tra religione e magia. Storia del prete modenese Guglielmo Campana [1460?-1541]*. Florence: Olschki, 1999). Campana's example and others indicate that the pre-Tridentine Catholic Church was anything but a monolith speaking with a single voice, but rather was a massive, heterogeneous institution encompassing many different beliefs and practices.

As for the other Modenese "witches," the majority were, as was true across Europe, women; they outnumbered men three to one. They tended to come from the lowest orders of society, frequently were widows or spinsters; and a fair number worked as prostitutes. Certain families specialized in the magical arts, creating veritable dynasties of witches and sorcerers. The witches' and sorcerers' clients were as rich and varied as the reasons for which they turned to those with access to the supernatural. Shopkeepers, lawyers, and peasants all sought assistance in order to uncover hidden treasures, to cure sick children, or to cause others to fall hopelessly and uncontrollably in love.

We know about this earlier culture war because the inquisitors kept very good records. The caches of trial transcripts maintained by inquisitorial commissions across the Italian peninsula are one of the most valuable sources available to historians. Not only do these records offer insight into the methods, concerns, and ideas of the men (they were all men) who sought to purify society by rooting out heresy (which is how they defined witchcraft); but even more valuably they provide a glimpse, however fleeting, into the fears, hopes, and aspirations of women and men, many of whom were illiterate, who would otherwise have disappeared completely from the historical record. However, the sides in these inquisitorial contests were terribly mismatched. Before the boards of judges who were expertly trained in legal procedures and matters of theology and diabolical possession, stood frightened defendants, illiterate in Latin and usually of much lower social rank, who were threatened with or actually subject to torture. That they responded at all, and that we still have access to their voices, is nothing short of miraculous.

In order to give readers the opportunity to hear these voices for themselves, Duni has appended to this study translations of parts of the trials of seven men and women who were accused of witchcraft and sorcery. For the first time, readers have access (mediated as they are by the sixteenth-century scribes who recorded the proceedings and by Duni's twenty-first-century translations) to the words and ideas of, among others, Bernardina Stadera, Sebastiano della Seca, Orsolina, nicknamed "the Red," and even the wizard-priest Don Campana. The inquisitors are represented as well by the questions they put to the defendants. Thus readers can witness for themselves some minor skirmishes in this early modern culture war.

Dennis Romano
Professor of History and Fine Arts
Syracuse University

ACKNOWLEDGEMENTS

Like most scholarly endeavors, this book has been the product of a collective effort in which the author, though alone responsible for the end result, has greatly benefited from the help, assistance and encouragement of many people.

Barbara Deimling, Director of Syracuse University in Florence, has been the "prime mover" of this project. Her firm commitment to publish such a book in the Villa Rossa Series and her tireless entreaties to have it published sooner rather than later are the first and main reason these pages are seeing the light.

I owe the greatest scholarly debt to Antonio Rotondò, my teacher and mentor from the times of my undergraduate studies at the University of Florence until his death this year. He has been, and will always be for me, a model of both intellectual rigor and generosity. It was he who introduced me to the study of early modern magic and of its repression, and to that extraordinarily rich trove of documents, the Inquisition archives of Modena. I first got to "know" many of the witches and wizards the reader will meet in this book in the course of Prof. Rotondò's unforgettable seminars, in which I learned how to read and analyze such fascinating texts.

Several friends were generous of their time, and their advice and moral support has helped me throughout the project. Special thanks to Sara Matthews-Grieco who was—as usual—a superlative first reader, whose countless suggestions were invaluable to the improvement of both the prose and the contents. Dennis Romano kindly wrote an insightful preface. Molly Bourne reviewed with acumen the captions for the images. Dinora Corsi provided me with very helpful suggestions on several specific points, while Lorenzo Fabbri and Lucia Felici lent ready ears to the periodic lamentations of a frustrated author.

The community of the "witch-hunters," near and far, looked on my undertaking with a sympathetic eye, and the encouragement of Stuart Clark, William Eamon, David Gentilcore, Richard Golden, Tamar Herzig, José Pedro Paiva, Walter Stephens, and Michaela Valente was the ideal stimulus I needed to keep working on the manuscript.

I was fortunate enough to receive a fellowship from Harvard University Center for Italian Renaissance Studies at Villa I Tatti in Florence, where most of the writing of the book was carried out. In that idyllic setting the Director, Joseph Connors, the interim Director Katharine Park, and the staff—especially Michael Rocke and the librarians—greatly eased my task. The friendship and support of the fellows and scholars made the year spent at I Tatti a truly memorable one, and it is a great pleasure to remember and thank the wonderful group of 2004-05.

Brenda Cooke at Syracuse University in Florence gave the book its elegant and beautiful design. Amanda George's sharpness as an editor was matched only by her sense of humor; Dorothea Barrett promptly answered my queries about the mysteries of the English language. Alexandra Korey was a very efficient "image hunter," and Anne Proctor took good care of the index of names.

It only remains for me to give to my wife Sandra, and my daughter Arianna, the most heartfelt *grazie* for having kept up with the distractions and absences that writing a book always involves, but most of all for having helped me to keep work and family in a healthy balance. To them I lovingly dedicate this book.

Under the Devil's Spell
Witches, Sorcerers, and the Inquisition
in Renaissance Italy

BETWEEN THE FIFTEENTH AND THE SEVENTEENTH CENTURIES, A WAVE of fear and violence gripped Europe. In all the most socially and culturally advanced countries, the intellectual and political elites, largely at the prompting of the Catholic Church, denounced the deadly threat to society and Christianity which came from men and women who were believed to have allied themselves with the devil. These individuals were learned magicians who were thought to be able to conjure up demons and witches, human beings who had purportedly made a pact with Satan and become his servants. Thus began the age of the witch-hunts.

During a period of almost three centuries, all over the Continent, courts both secular and ecclesiastical brought to trial people whose personal characteristics—social and marital status, gender, occupation—made them stand out as likely allies of the devil. Many of them were simple folk-healers, in charge of curing people and cattle alike with herbal remedies and spells, or "wise women" who delivered babies, cared for infants, and fixed shaky marriages with charms and prayers. They all paid the price of being associated with Satan, and were condemned for crimes that are regarded today as purely imaginary.

We now know the contours of this disturbing page of European history substantially better than just a few decades ago. Thorough and accurate research carried out in the last twenty years has given us a much more precise idea of both the geographical and the quantitative dimensions of the witch-hunts. It is currently estimated that over one hundred thousand women and men were tried (and often tortured), mostly in the countries of north-western Europe: France, the German-speaking world, Switzerland, Scandinavia, and Britain. At least half of those tried were put to death.

Appalling as these figures are, the witch-hunts were not the "holocaust" some hasty scholars claimed had taken the life of five million people. They did not affect all parts of the Continent in the same way, as some were hardly touched. They targeted men as well as women, although the latter were accused and condemned in greater numbers: about three-quarters of all "witches" who appeared in court were in fact women. Although this information has become widely available in recent years, old misconceptions still linger among the general public, propagated and kept alive by the mass media, from best-selling fiction to blockbuster movies. The witch-hunts are often attributed to the "dark ages," a chronologically undefined period associated with vague ideas of cultural backwardness. They bring to mind gruesome images of unrestrained torture, and of course the power of the Inquisition, a tribunal that embodies a Kafkian nightmare of secrecy, arbitrariness, and gratuitous cruelty.[1]

Granted, the legal systems of the fifteenth and sixteenth centuries were hardly sensitive to human rights issues, and the Inquisition did resort systematically to torture. But if we look at witchcraft trials under this light only, they will tell us solely of the context that generated them: the political and religious establishment and its fears, its repressive tools, its efforts to crush any culture or group that seemed to threaten the status quo. Such a perspective will yield no meaningful information about the hunts' victims, their mentality, their lives. In the past, historians who adopted such a one-sided approach usually expressed the strongest contempt, mixed with feelings of cultural superiority, for the blinding prejudice of theologians and judges. More recently, other "scholars" fill in the spaces supposedly left empty after the annihilation of the beliefs of our ancestors by projecting unto the past twentieth and twenty-first century ideas of traditional culture, thus recreating a "lost world" which is actually a mirror reflection of current trends and fads. The surge of interest for the worship of the "goddess," the mythical, age-old Euro-Asian religion, is the case in point: fascinated by this idea, many regard medieval and early modern "witches" as persecuted followers of this supposedly universal cult, whose features are fancifully reconstructed as an ancient version of vaguely new-age ideals.

Such stereotyped views of the witch-hunts and their protagonists have long been rejected by social and cultural historians, who have given us an infinitely more accurate and articulate knowledge of both the "witches'" world and of their persecutors' agenda and tools. The present book, while obviously drawing on these findings, does not have the ambition of discussing the phenomenon in its entire geographical and chronological dimensions, nor from all its viewpoints.[2] Its aim is to contribute to our understanding of magic and witchcraft and of its repression in one specific area, over a relatively short period of time:

the northern states of the Italian peninsula during the Renaissance, that is, from the early fourteenth to the end of the sixteenth century. The nuanced and varied picture of the beliefs and practices that can be derived from archival sources will show how recourse to magic was not solely the affair of sorceresses or conjurers, but an integral part of Renaissance Italians' everyday life. Practitioners of magic, as a matter of fact, while sometimes socially at the margins of communities, were often relatively well-established if not prominent individuals: priests, for instance, figured very frequently among those evoking demons or casting spells. The similarities between, and the mixing of, magical techniques and Catholic ritual, so strikingly highlighted by Inquisition trials, will help explain such an apparently surprising fact, as well as demonstrate the contradictory efforts by the Catholic Church's author-ities to repress abuses of its rites while keeping faith in their quasi-mag-ical efficacy intact.

Choosing the Italian peninsula in the Renaissance to examine the phenomenon of the witch-craze is predicated on a number of conditions particular to this place and time. The Italian states were economically, politically, and especially culturally, the most advanced on the Continent. Although many Italian theologians and prominent Church figures believed firmly in the threat represented by magic and witch-craft, they were challenged by a strong intellectual movement that con-sidered the witches' tales little more than harmless dreams. Between the second half of the fifteenth and the first decades of the sixteenth century jurists, physicians, and theologians argued that the witches' supposed feats were to be blamed on their weak minds, upset by the devil's delusory powers. In the same period some of the most presti-gious thinkers were busy reworking magic into a legitimate, and actu-ally fundamental, component of scientific and religious discourse, free-ing it from negative connotations.[3] On the Italian peninsula, then, the witch-hunters' paranoia did not enjoy the kind of absolute hegemony it is credited with by some superficial reconstructions.

Atypical when compared to the majority of the other European coun-tries, the Italian states also provide a case in point to show how repres-sive institutions and their policies could be far from monolithic. After a head-start in the last quarter of the fifteenth century, both the secular courts and the papal Inquisition substantially slowed down the hunt for witches. This was largely replaced—in the case of the Inquisition—by the frantic search for Italian Protestants in the central decades of the sixteenth century. When eventually witchcraft came back to center stage after the Council of Trent, the revamped Roman Inquisition approached it with an unexpected caution and restraint, which prevented the outbreak of large-scale witch-hunts on the north European model.

At a time in which thousands of witches were burned at the stake elsewhere on the Continent, the substantial lack of interest on the part of the Italian magistrates cannot be fully understood without taking into consideration the intellectual framework of the inquisitors, as well as the overall goals of the Inquisition's policy. It is for this reason that the first chapter of the book starts by examining the theological and legal principles on which the condemnation of magic rested, as well as providing an overview of the process that brought the witch, the human ally of the devil, to displace the magician as the main enemy of Christianity at the end of the fifteenth century. Due attention is devoted also to the structure of the Inquisition, the tools at the disposal of its judges, and especially its activity in the north of the Italian peninsula. Our knowledge on this last aspect, although fragmentary especially for its earlier phase, enables us to get a sense of the changes that the tribunal's policy and organization went through over the centuries, thus dispelling the old stereotype of the Inquisition as an ageless institution. It will be particularly interesting to understand how and why the rhythm of the witch-hunts in the Italian states shifted quite dramatically between the late fifteenth and the late sixteenth century. From a steady increase climaxing in numerous large and bloody witch-hunts at the beginning of the fifteen hundreds, the prosecution of witchcraft went through a quick and drastic decline in the central decades of the century, and finally entered a third and final phase in which both witches and magicians, although tried by judges in great numbers, saw their punishments often reduced to mere spiritual penances.

In the second chapter the focus will shift to the actual beliefs and practices of magicians and sorceresses, as revealed by the rich archival files of the Italian Inquisitions. Surprisingly, "witches" will here be in the minority, as their feats—enabled by the devil—appear seldom in the surviving documents. Rather, the reader will be struck by the ubiquitous presence of magic in the everyday life of early modern Italian cities. The extremely wide spectrum of practices described in the trials of individuals accused of witchcraft speaks of both the diverse cultural traditions that shaped current beliefs, and the variety of goals pursued by means of magic. Magical techniques belonging to the realm of folklore were frequently mixed with suggestions coming from the world of high culture, or vice versa, through channels and agents that are fascinating to trace. This is an avenue that opens a window onto another key issue of this second chapter, that is, how culturally and socially heterogeneous was the pool of those who practiced magic. Resorting to supernatural forces provided an opportunity for women and men from all walks of life to mingle, exchanging knowledge gleaned from their respective backgrounds. Books of magic, sometimes printed but often handwritten by expert magicians, not only changed hands, but were also used as compensation for advice received. In this way the apparently separated dimensions of written and oral culture came in contact with one another, revealing how complex their interplay could be in the early modern period.

The large appendix of archival documents—here published in English for the first time—provides the reader with insights into a multifaceted world of individuals trying, at different levels, to cope with life's misadventures through magical means. At the same time, it introduces the mental world of inquisitors, showing what logic was at work behind the judges' decisions. This selection of documents is meant to convey a sense of the richness of data that can be extracted from inquisitorial files. Social, cultural, gender history issues are here highlighted in trial records that recount the deeds of Renaissance practitioners of magic from the most diverse backgrounds.

All the documents come from the archives of the Inquisition tribunal of the northern Italian city of Modena, the second city in size and importance in the duchy ruled by the Este family from the capital of Ferrara (Fig. 1). Modena was conveniently situated on the Via Emilia, since Roman times the main route connecting Bologna and the Romagna, to the south-east, to Milan and Lombardy in the north-west, while a close network of rivers and canals provided communication with Ferrara and with the main waterway of the whole northern part of the Italian peninsula, the Po river. This strategic location was certainly one of the reasons for the city's prosperity and growth in the middle ages and the Renaissance, largely due to silk and wool production and trade. Enduring and close relations with its fertile countryside, which provided most of the staple products for the inhabitants, contributed to sustain a population numbering approximately between 10,000 and 15,000 inhabitants in the sixteenth century. In the early fifteen hundreds Modena was shaken by the catastrophic series of wars that ravaged the entire peninsula, and found itself a pawn between powerful contenders such as the Holy Roman Empire and the papacy. Stability returned only in the 1530s, but another momentous conflict, which pitted the Este against the papacy, brought the elevation of the city to state capital in 1598. As the ruling family moved in, so did their government papers, thus making the present State Archives in Modena one of the most important in Italy.

Those archives are particularly valuable also in that they are practically the only ones in Italy to include a series of Inquisition records stretching from the late medieval period through the eighteenth century, thus spanning (although with large gaps in the early phase) a good portion of the institutional life of this Church tribunal. The Modenese files are comparatively less well known than those of Venice which, although equally rich, were produced by a particular, local version of the Inquisition, perhaps less representative than that of Modena in terms of the Inquisition's policies and attitudes. Finally, the wealth of the archival series preserved in Modena—and the moderate dimension of that city—make the reconstruction of the identities of sorceresses and magicians easier than in other contexts.

A first-hand encounter with primary sources seems to the present author the best way to get a fresh sense of the complexity and variety of themes offered by witchcraft studies—a field that cuts across many different research focuses—as well as a means to avoid stereotypes and simplifications of historical reality. The hope is that this book will achieve both goals.

CHAPTER I

THE FOUNDATIONS
OF THE WITCH-HUNT

Medieval Condemnations of Magic and Sorcery

Theologians and Magicians

THE PHILOSOPHERS, THEOLOGIANS, AND LAWYERS WHO DEALT WITH the issue of witchcraft during the Renaissance period had a solid intellectual framework to refer to, and cope with, in their search for answers to the new, troubling issue of the sect of the witches. During the centuries of the late middle ages (between the twelfth and the four-teenth, especially) intellectuals—mostly Catholic clergy—had investi-gated in depth the nature of magic, that is, of the occult powers that enabled some men and women to influence and modify things in the physical world in a supernatural way. These thinkers had tried to under-stand the extent and the limits of these powers, believed to have been established by God, to ascertain what results were achievable through natural means, and what could only be wrought through the help of the devil. Although late medieval thought dealt with magic—as opposed to the later concept of diabolical witchcraft—its impact on later develop-ments was to be great. As witches were supposed to be able to harm or heal magically, the medieval treatises provided the "scientific proof" of the connection between the practice of most kinds of magic and the demonic world, thus demonstrating that all magicians, and by exten-sion all witches, had very likely consorted with the devil, and were to be punished accordingly.

Thomas Aquinas (circa 1225-74), the most influential philosopher of the entire middle ages, had attentively examined the theories of learned magician-philosophers, who claimed to be able to work wonders thanks to the effects of the heavenly bodies and the occult properties of plants, animals, talismans, and spells. Although he admitted the possi-bility that natural forces may occultly produce a variety of phenomena, he pointed to the equal possibility that demons could achieve similar results, thus making it virtually impossible to distinguish what was obtained through natural magic from that which was silently worked by evil spirits. In any case, Aquinas sternly affirmed that most magicians' feats could be accomplished solely through the intervention of a super-human being, who, given the evil nature of most of the magicians' operations, could only be the devil. Furthermore, he pointed out that any human attempt at communicating with demons to obtain their assistance implied some form of compact between the two parties, and thus heresy on the part of the magician since he (or she) was choosing to collaborate with Satan, thereby rejecting God. This was the root of the concept of the pact between the witch and the devil, which was destined to be the cornerstone of all theories on diabolical witchcraft.[1]

In the course of the fourteenth century, the growing fascination with the occult arts among educated Europeans was fed by the diffusion of a large body of works on philosophical, astrological, and magical themes. Most of them were the product of a complex fusion of different cultural traditions—Greco-Roman, Jewish, and Islamic—that had taken place in the Arab world between the ninth and the twelfth centuries. From the twelfth century onwards these books, translated into Latin, contributed greatly to the revival of European culture, raising however numerous questions. Astrology figured prominently among the topics treated by this literature, but in many texts the emphasis was not so much on how the path of stars and planets could show the future course of events, but rather on the relationship between the heavenly and the earthly spheres. It was believed that a deep knowledge of the connections linking the earth to the higher heavens could enable humans to produce wondrous effects through the manipulation of the hidden properties of the natural world, activated by celestial influences.

The surge of interest in the occult that swept Europe in the late middle ages prompted increasingly stiff rejections of magic from Church authorities. In 1398 the faculty of theology of the University of Paris, the most prestigious in Europe at the time, issued a categorical condemnation of all magical operations, including *maleficium* (harmful magic). This was therefore one of the first documents to define the widespread, lower-class practice of sorcery (that included malevolent as well as beneficent magic) as a diabolical endeavor, thus greatly expanding the range of magical operations that could be prosecuted as heretical based on their association with the devil.[2]

Not all voices were in accordance with these positions, however. During the fifteenth century, as a matter of fact, an influential school of thought developed, whose proponents re-evaluated magic in its learned, "purest" form as a perfectly legitimate way to acquire information about—and manipulate—the universe. Fostered by the climate of cultural change that characterized the Italian states during the Renaissance, this bold new way of defining magic doubtless had a considerable impact on the attitude of the elites towards witches and witchcraft.

By this time, both ecclesiastical and lay courts had been trying magicians and sorceresses for more than a century, and it is to this legal framework that we must now turn.

The legal status of magic was peculiar, since it could be regarded as a crime by both secular and ecclesiastical courts. As it often involved causing harm to people or goods, its practice had been the target of secular laws and courts throughout the early middle ages. At the same time, its questionable nature as a skill or knowledge possibly linked to demonic intervention in the material world made it an activity on which the Catholic Church kept a very vigilant eye. Jurists, therefore, defined the practice of magic a crime of "mixed jurisdiction," meaning that both state and Church courts could prosecute it.[3]

From the beginning, the legal treatment of magic was shaped by laws issued by Roman emperors converted to Christianity, prohibiting any form of magic under pain of death.[4] In the high middle ages the growth of Church law, known as canon law, also included discussions of sorcery and divination. This is the case for the *Decretum*, the most important collection of Church laws compiled by the Bolognese Master Gratian around 1140, which calls for both excommunication and exile for unrepentant magicians. At the same time, Gratian included in his compilation an earlier law, the canon *Episcopi* (circa ninth century), which dismissed as unreal current tales of women who allegedly rode at night following a female goddess. Thanks to its authoritativeness, this document was destined to be one of the main obstacles to emerging theories of witchcraft, which asserted the reality of the witches' ride to their meeting with the devil.[5]

The revival of Roman law that took place in Europe from the twelfth century brought the legal provisions of Italian city-states in line with the severity of the Roman emperors' edicts against magicians. In most towns, municipal codes and statutes prescribed that such crimes receive capital punishment. The repression of magic and sorcery—as that of most other crimes—became increasingly effective following an important change in the legal systems of several European countries, also due to the growing influence of Roman law: a new trial procedure was introduced, called "inquisitorial" to distinguish it from its predecessor, the earlier medieval "accusatorial" procedure.[6] In the new system, adopted by both secular and ecclesiastical tribunals from the thirteenth century onwards, legal action could be initiated not only on the basis of an accusation brought forth by a private individual, but also on the basis of simple rumors or other information obtained by the officers of the court, who cumulated the powers of a prosecutor to those of a trial judge. Precise rules clarified that judges should conduct separate and confidential interrogations of accusers, of the accused, and of witnesses. Written records had to be kept of all proceedings, and any evidence acquired by such means should be evaluated rationally so as to establish whether the defendant was guilty or not.

Particularly important were the standards of proof introduced in the inquisitorial system: it was required that, in order for a guilty verdict to be reached, defendants had to be accused by either two eyewitnesses who had seen the crime being committed, or by the accused's own confession. In the case of witchcraft, the first requirement was extremely difficult to fulfill, since usually there were no witnesses to the witches' meeting with the devil or to the casting of spells. Under these circumstances, confession was practically the only proof obtainable—and necessary—to condemn someone.

Given the importance of confessions and the obvious reticence of defendants, the new trial procedure provided one powerful tool to put pressure on the accused: recourse to judicial torture (Fig. 2). Judges could torture suspects in order to elicit confessions, and thus obtain the evidence required to bring trials to their conclusion. Although a detailed set of rules limited the use of torture in the courtroom, their application depended on individual judges, therefore leaving plenty of room for violations. Indiscriminate and exceedingly heavy sessions of torture would evidently bend the will of even the most resistant, steering the defendants' confessions in the direction desired by the court. Judges often used torture to confirm their suspicions, and did not refrain from asking the defendants leading questions. The impact of this was especially notable in crimes of heresy, which were normally limited to the mental sphere, as well as in those of witchcraft, whose details and very existence were often inseparable from the prosecutors' ideas about them. The abuses of torture, and systematic leading questioning of suspects, provided judges with confessions that not only "proved" the accuracy of their suspicions in specific cases, but also confirmed current demonological theories about certain criminal groups—heretics, magicians, and, finally, witches. At the same time, information obtained in the torture chamber was incorporated in the growing body of scholarship about these enemies of Christendom, thus shaping leading questions asked by judges in different places and times, and eventually making a fundamental contribution to the spread of the belief in a new heretical sect of the witches.[7]

In the meantime, a new ecclesiastical court, the Inquisition, was created.[8] Exclusively devoted to the repression of heresy, the Inquisition sparked the production of a new type of legal literature, the handbooks for inquisitors: these defined with increasing precision what constituted heretical behavior or belief, and were particularly important for their treatment of magical practices. The most popular of such works, the *Directorium Inquisitorum* (*Handbook of the Inquisitors*, 1376) written by the Catalan inquisitor Nicolau Eymeric, asserted that magicians were to be considered heretics if they had invoked the devil and had honored him with offerings, as in a religious cult, since this would be idolatry. But even if no act of formal worship had occurred, the simple fact of applying to the devil (as opposed to praying to God) to accomplish something could, if certain conditions were fulfilled, be considered apostasy from the faith, and therefore heresy.[9] Contrary to earlier, softer treatments, this equation between magic and heresy resulted in the consignment of the condemned to secular authorities for execution, in the case of an unrepentant or relapsed (i.e. second-time offender) heretic. The cooperation between Church and states to punish sorcerers was strengthened by the gradual inclusion of magic, and eventually witchcraft, as a form of heresy, in the category of crimes of exceptional gravity (*crimina excepta*) that had first been applied to high treason. In such cases, courts could suspend traditional guarantees to the accused because the horrendous nature of the crime required that its repression be as swift and ruthless as possible.[10]

The Birth of the Witch

The first decades of the fifteenth century witnessed a significant shift in theories about magic and sorcery. Theologians and inquisitors who had originally acknowledged the heretical status of magic—as based on demonic intervention—increasingly began to see magicians as worshippers of the devil in a sort of alternative religion. It was believed that those who practiced demonic magic and sorcery did so not as isolated agents, but rather collectively and cooperatively, attending large nocturnal meetings where horrible acts of orgiastic sex, cannibalism, and profanation of the sacraments were committed in the presence of Satan himself. These "sabbats," as the gatherings were called (with a word whose Jewish origin had already been used to discredit the meetings of other unorthodox groups), were the key feature of a new type of diabolical sorcery, witchcraft, which a growing number of influential Church leaders came to see as constituting a grave danger for Christianity. For these churchmen, the devil was trying to enroll in his army as many witches as possible, especially women but also men, providing them with the ability to injure magically. Satan's master plan aimed at causing the perdition of the faithful and the destruction of humankind.[11]

Several factors account for the rise of this extraordinary new conspiracy theory. Following the dramatic split of the Catholic Church known as the Great Schism (1378-1417), there was a sense that such deeply troubling events were the product of a growing demonic presence in the world. As a consequence, religious leaders felt the urge to reform both devotional behavior and ecclesiastical institutions. Popular "superstitions"—meaning a variety of magical operations performed by individuals of low social status—were seen increasingly as facets of one single type of heretical behavior, characterized by the connection of their practitioners with the devil. In the meantime, in the struggle against the heresies that challenged the religious establishment during the first half of the fifteenth century (as for example the Bohemian Hussites), Church authorities and theologians started propagating the idea that heretical groups had constituted literally an anti-Church, with its own perverted rituals, based in the end on the rejection of Christ and the glorification of Satan. Those who practiced magic of any kind were the most dangerous perpetrators of the diabolical plot: considered witches, they were a novel embodiment of the frightening image of the heretic as a member of the fifth column, the human ally of the Enemy of humankind.[12]

The alarm against witchcraft gained momentum quickly. Between the 1430s and the 1460s, an impressive series of works, many by Dominican friars and inquisitors (Johannes Nider, Jean Vineti, Nicolas Jacquier, Girolamo Visconti) and some by other clergy or lay intellectuals (among several others Pierre Mamoris and Claude Tholosan, this latter a lay judge) gave the first detailed descriptions of the witches and their deeds.[13] The fundamental features of witchcraft, as defined by these and later theologians, were three: first, the pact with the devil, a formal act through which humans surrendered their souls to Satan and received in exchange magical powers; second, the sabbat, the night meeting of all witches to worship the devil and perform obscene and blasphemous rites; third, the ability of the witches to fly, both to attend the sabbat in far away places and to return to their homes unseen. These elements were a combination of medieval learned theories on magicians and their connection with the devil, Catholic polemics against

heterodox groups and their rituals, and age-old folkloric beliefs and traditions seen through the suspicious eyes of theologians and inquisitors
unaware of (and uninterested in) their genuine meaning. All these elements came together largely as a result of Inquisition trials of heretics
and magicians, and formed an extremely coherent and resistant theory,
which lasted for more than two centuries and is referred to usually as
the "cumulative concept" of witchcraft.[14]

The three main characteristics—pact, sabbat, flight—were accompanied by a combination of other lurid details that were not central to the
cumulative concept (Figs. 3-10). For example, the description of what
happened during the sabbat could include the ritual infanticide of
unbaptized babies and the use of their bodies to concoct maleficent
unguents (Fig. 5), the profanation of Christian sacraments and symbols
(Fig. 4), the sexual intercourse of the male and female witches with
demons in human or animal form (Figs. 9-10). Likewise, there was
never general agreement on the witches' supposed ability to transform
themselves into animals to commit certain crimes. (Fig. 7)

Regardless of these variants, however, the new theory on witchcraft
placed a particular emphasis on the corporeal nature of the contacts
between demons and humans. Expanding on Aquinas' theory of the
"virtual" body which demons could assume to interact with mortals,
fifteenth-century theologians insisted that witches met the devil and his
minions truly and bodily. This, they argued, sharply distinguished
witches of their time from the women mentioned in the canon *Episcopi*,
whose nocturnal experiences, similar as they may have seemed to the
sabbat, were simply dreams and visions. The substantial rejection of
the earlier skeptical approach expressed by canon law went together
with a sense of the novelty of witchcraft, which according to these
authors had first appeared at the beginning of their century. "Modern"
witches, especially female, coupled the ability to cast maleficent spells,
always typical of uncultured sorceresses, with that of meeting the devil
face to face, that up to then had been thought to be exclusive to (male)
learned magicians.[15] Witches, however, were not Satan's masters, as
learned magicians claimed to be and, unlike these latter, their contact with
the devil could frequently be sexual.

Repressive theory and judicial practice went hand in hand. Papal condemnations of diabolical witchcraft, theological treatises expounding
its features, and popular sermons warning against this danger mirrored
and reinforced the activity of tribunals, both lay and ecclesiastical, in
the uprooting of the new heresy. As early as 1427 the greatly popular

Franciscan preacher Bernardino of Siena delivered in his hometown a series of fiery sermons against sorcery in general, denouncing in particular the witches who supposedly transformed themselves into cats by using an unguent made of the bodies of children they had killed, and urged the faithful to report to the Inquisition anybody guilty of such crimes.[16] Several official papal letters—referred to as Bulls—testify to the growing concern raised by the new witches: first Alexander V in 1409, then Eugenius IV in 1434 and again in 1437, finally Innocent VIII in 1484, denounced the existence of men and women who, through a pact made with the devil, had received the ability to perform all sorts of demonic sorcery, and gave full powers to the Inquisition to prosecute them with all due urgency.[17] Recent research has shown that early witchcraft trials originated precisely from the territories to whose inquisitors these letters had been addressed: a fairly small area in the western Alps region, between France, Italy, and Switzerland, starting from the 1420s.[18] In the next four decades the witch-craze spread to a substantially wider area between the Mediterranean and the German-speaking world: the northern regions of the Italian peninsula (present-day Piedmont, Lombardy, and Trentino), the southeastern parts of France, the central and western cantons of Switzerland, and the south-western regions of Germany.

The tools that the inquisitorial system provided judges with were to prove decisive in increasing the number of witchcraft prosecutions. The torture of suspected witches, to whom a favorable treatment was promised in exchange for cooperation with the court, yielded not only elaborate descriptions of crimes and rituals, but also long lists of names of accomplices, people who supposedly had been at the sabbat and had shared the affiliation with the devil. These men and women, tried and tortured in due course, would invariably become a precious source of information about still other witches. In this way single trials could ignite a powerful reaction, resulting in the prosecution of tens, sometimes hundreds and even thousands, of witches—although truly large-scale witch-hunts did not occur before the last years of the sixteenth century. The number of trials in some of the regions mentioned, reached already significant levels between the late 1470s and 1480s.[19]

In that same period, the single most important book on witchcraft was published, the *Malleus Maleficarum* (*Hammer of the Witches*), first printed in 1487.[20] Its author was the German Heinrich Krämer, a Dominican inquisitor destined to a significant—and very controversial—career as a witch-hunter. Three years earlier, Krämer had received from Pope Innocent VIII the mandate to proceed against witches in a wide area going from Salzburg, in Austria, to the northern German city of Bremen: his experience on the job was distilled into his "magnum opus".[21] Much lengthier than any previous treatment of the topic, the *Malleus Maleficarum* presented a painstaking discussion of all the elements that composed the stereotypical image of the witch, backing every argument with a wealth of authorities (classical as well as religious) that lent great weight to the thesis of the reality of witchcraft, and furnished professional readers, especially inquisitors, with a detailed guidebook to the legal procedure against witches.

Particularly significant was the author's insistence on the evil nature of the female sex. The western tradition of misogyny, of which this book provides an impressive, if unoriginal, compendium, lent Krämer an important argument to link women and demons, and to solidify forever the image of the witch as that of a woman. Weaker beings than men, he argued, women were readier to fall prey to Satan's temptations and, as they were also more carnal than men, they could satisfy their lust only by consorting sexually with "incubi" demons—that is, demons with male sexual attributes. These latter could thus make female witches pregnant using the semen they had previously received through sex with men as "succubi," or female, demons. In this way, through both temptation of the flesh and procreation, the devil had found a way to make his adepts proliferate. As a consequence, God grew angrier at humans for their sins—which resulted in more freedom left to the devil to tempt Christians, in a frightening vicious circle that threatened to swallow all of humankind (Figs. 10 and 14).

Although none of these arguments was new, the thoroughness and convenience of a single-volume treatment of witchcraft made the *Malleus Maleficarum* a real best-seller, going through thirteen editions between 1487 and 1520 (and sixteen more between 1574 and 1669) in various cities all over Europe. The success of the book firmly established the concept of witchcraft as a conspiratorial type of demonic magic, practiced by renegade Christians who had abandoned God for the devil and had created a sort of ever-growing anti-society. Furthermore, by placing an unprecedented emphasis on the female sex's evil nature as the factor that explained why witches were predominantly women, the *Malleus Maleficarum* made an invaluable contribution towards making witchcraft a decidedly "sex-related" crime: it is currently estimated that about seventy-five percent of all people prosecuted for this offence were women.[22]

Although the witch-hunters' theories enjoyed widespread support from the highest levels in the Catholic Church as well as from lay officials and governments all over Europe, opposition to them remained strong and often open throughout the medieval and Renaissance periods. A heterogeneous front of theologians, philosophers, physicians, and jurists—many coming from Italian states—never ceased urging caution and voicing doubts, if not outright disbelief, in matters relating to witchcraft.

The key document virtually all witchcraft skeptics referred to was the already mentioned canon *Episcopi*, an early medieval (circa ninth century) Church law erroneously thought to be the ruling of a much older Council of Ancyra (314 AD), which was revered as a very authoritative source.[23] This law, while acknowledging the reality of harmful magic, dismissed as dreams and visions (created by the devil) the nocturnal experiences of those "wicked women," who claimed to ride for long distances following the pagan goddess Diana (Fig. 11). The author of *Episcopi*, as we clearly understand today, was describing and condemning the vestiges of some pre-Christian religious cult still alive in Carolingian Europe;[24] but fifteenth- and sixteenth-century thinkers thought this law referred to the vexed question of their day, the sect of the witches and their night ride to the sabbat. Witchcraft skeptics argued—to the protests of the inquisitors—that modern witches were deluded by the devil exactly like the old followers of Diana, and that therefore everything they purportedly did and saw at the demonic meetings was only a mental vision.

Significantly, such reservations were widespread even among orthodox theologians, such as the German Dominican Johannes Nider or the Spanish Alphonsus de Spina, who admitted that witches' experiences could sometimes be purely imaginary.[25] More radical was the stance taken by intellectuals who, in the climate of cultural change created by Renaissance humanism in the Italian states, argued against mainstream scholasticism that the very nature of demons made witchcraft impossible. This was the case with the Augustinian monk Guglielmo Becchi, bishop of Fiesole and friend to Lorenzo de' Medici, author of a work which asserted that demons did not have any physical body, and therefore were unable to have any material contact with humans.[26]

Following this lead, several prominent jurists wrote to show the legal difficulties encountered in, and the care necessary for, the prosecution of witchcraft cases. In the second half of the fifteenth century, Ambrogio Vignati and Ulrich Molitor (the first a professor of law at Turin, the second a Swiss lawyer who had studied in Pavia) expressed serious doubts on the possibility of many feats attributed to the witches—from the flight to the sabbat to animal metamorphosis.[27] Both Vignati and the Franciscan Samuele de Cassini also contested the reality of witchcraft with theological arguments, stressing that God's omnipotence and love towards humankind excluded that He would give the devil free rein so as to enable the witches to carry out such nefarious crimes.[28]

At the beginning of the sixteenth century a harsh controversy pitted lawyer Giovanni Francesco Ponzinibio, from Piacenza, against the Dominican theologian Bartolomeo Spina, inquisitor of Modena.[29] In his *De Lamiis* (circa 1520) Ponzinibio argued, based on the canon *Episcopi*, that all of the witches' supposed experiences were actually due to the devil's great delusory skills. Admitting that the so-called witches were mostly rough country people of low social and moral level—especially women—Ponzinibio interestingly turned this argument in his favor, claiming that their words could not be trusted in court. Since witchcraft was impossible and its alleged protagonists were deluded and degraded countryfolk, he concluded polemically, inquisitors not only had to refuse to proceed against the witches, but should actually prosecute those who believed in the reality of the sabbat.

Ponzinibio was furiosly attacked by Spina, author of *Quaestio de Strigibus* (*The Problem of the Witches*, 1523) to which he eventually appended a *Quadruplex Apologia de Lamiis in Ponzinibium* (*Fourfold Defence on Witches Against Ponzinibio*, 1525). Spina first demolished the authoritativeness of *Episcopi*, casting serious doubts on its orthodoxy. With a typically circular argument, he then stressed that the reality of witchcraft was proved not only by innumerable confessions from witches, all identical and mutually supportive, but especially by the unanimous opinion of theologians, holy doctors of the Church, and popes. Sensing that Ponzinibio's thesis was potentially devastating on the legal level—as it could have altogether prevented the prosecution of witchcraft—Spina urged all inquisitors to try the lawyer as a heretic, and to burn him and his work, so filled with errors and impiety.

Such a violent tone, however, did not apparently frighten critics, since in those same years the Milanese Andrea Alciato, eventually one of the most prestigious jurists in Europe, was writing in support of a skeptical stance.[30] Around 1516, called to give his advice on a large witch-hunt in the Alpine areas of Lombardy, Alciato decidedly rejected the claim that some of the accused women were to be condemned just for having been at the sabbat. Affirming that the supposed demonic gathering was solely the product of mental delusions, he pointed to the physiological cause for these, to be found in a disease of the imagination already described by scientists and physicians from classical antiquity. Witches, he argued, were just poor deluded women, who needed to be "treated rather with hellebore than with the fire" of the stake (hellebore is a strong herbal medicine then thought to purify the body and the mind).

Alciato's opinion had a remarkable influence, both in Italy and abroad, on opponents of the witch-hunts such as Girolamo Cardano and Johann Wier (or Weyer). The first, a famous astrologer and mathematician from Milan, stressed in his *De Rerum Varietate* (1557) that witches were simply poor mountain women suffering from hallucinations due to their meager diet. Wier, a physician from the Brabant, was the author of one of the most important tracts on the subject to be published in the entire century, *De Praestigiis Daemonum* (1563). In it, drawing on Alciato and Cardano as well as on his own vast erudition, he argued for the pathological explanation of witchcraft, seen as an illusion experienced by women whose bodily "humors" are unbalanced and therefore upset their mental faculties.[31]

By the time Wier wrote his book, the witchcraft debate seemed to be increasingly dominated by intellectuals who did not come from the Italian states—from the French jurist Jean Bodin to the English country gentleman Reginald Scot, to the Swiss physician Thomas Erastus.[32] While works written on this issue by Italian thinkers became few and far apart, concerns about the devil's presence did not disappear from the Italian peninsula, but underwent a significant change. On the one hand, Italian inquisitors stepped up the prosecution of magical practices, substantially increasing the numbers of cases tried. On the other hand, they dealt with cases of witchcraft with growing caution and restraint, following strict guidelines issued by Roman authorities which seemingly had adopted some of the skeptics' ideas.

To understand the extent and the causes of these changes fully, however, we have first to consider more in detail the tribunal of the Inquisition, its structure and ideology, the pace of its activity, and to highlight the modifications these underwent particularly from the fourteenth to the sixteenth centuries.

The Inquisition in the Italian States in the Renaissance

Organization and Procedures in the Medieval Period

Although the repression of magic and witchcraft was by no means an exclusive prerogative of ecclesiastical courts, it is impossible to deny that both the definition of these "crimes" and the strong impulse to prosecute them was largely due to Church figures and institutions. Among these, the most important role was played by the "tribunal of the faith," that is, the Inquisition, and by its men, the inquisitors.

The Inquisition (from the Latin word "inquisitio," investigation) was instituted in the first decades of the thirteenth century by Roman pontiffs to make the repression of non-conformist religious ideas and movements speedier and more efficient, in a time in which heresy seemed to grow at a pace that threatened the Catholic Church's monopoly.[33] Given the apparent inadequacy of the bishops' tribunals—the normal judicial tool at the Church's disposal—to face this enemy, medieval popes, starting with Gregory IX (1227-41), began to appoint special judges delegate to repress heresy. This "papal Inquisition," as it is normally called, was thus not really a court system, but rather a task ("officium inquisitionis") entrusted to individual clergy, whom the pope had empowered to detect, try, and punish heretics autonomously. During these first centuries—and, as far as the northern Italian states are concerned, really until the middle of the sixteenth century—no single central institution existed to coordinate and oversee the workings of all the judges: that is why historians now consider it more appropriate to speak of single "inquisitors," rather than of "the Inquisition," for this earlier phase.[34] In this period the tribunal was very different from its later, more famous versions, such as the Roman, Portuguese, and especially Spanish Inquisitions (which came into being between the end of the fifteenth and the middle of the sixteenth century): all of these had a central board of supreme inquisitors who appointed local judges and then kept a very close eye on their activity, frequently correcting if not altogether overriding their decisions.[35]

Practically from the beginning inquisitors came mostly from the ranks of the newly created orders of friars, Franciscans and Dominicans, both with a strong emphasis on a militant brand of Catholicism, and—especially Dominicans—on preaching and solid theological training, which seemed the best systems to combat heresy. Chosen by the Ministers-General of the respective orders (and eventually appointed directly by them, rather than by the pope), the friar-judges were dispatched to the territories in which they were to carry out their duty.

The geographical extension of an inquisitor's jurisdiction could vary, but tended to overlap with that of the administrative unit of his order, the province. As provinces could be rather large, for instance grouping together several present-day Italian regions, inquisitors would often appoint vicars to perform their duty in certain parts of the province. The degree of autonomy which vicars enjoyed could be fairly high, but it did not normally include the power to torture nor to emit the final sentence of a trial: for both cases, either the chief inquisitor had to be present and in charge of the proceedings, or at least a written authorization from him had to be in the vicar's hands. This subordination required that vicars keep frequently in touch with their superiors, informing them of the state of ongoing trials and requesting suggestions or permissions.[36]

Inquisitors could, and frequently did, seek the advice of experts of law and theology, calling lawyers and fellow friars to consultation, whose results were not binding for the court.[37] In any case, no decision could be taken by the tribunal on grave issues—torture and sentence—without prior consultation with, and approval of, the local bishop, as established by a decree of the council of Vienne in 1317.[38] This rule was not always followed by inquisitors in the Italian states; yet, together with the other limitations mentioned, it shows that inquisitors were not completely free in the management of their tribunal, but had to cope with secular clergy (that is, clergy that was more involved with worldly matters), to whom most bishops belonged, and with lay people—the consultants. This could result in local pressures and concerns influencing the court, making the prosecution of heresy not always an easy task.

In the Italian peninsula, the trial procedure of the tribunal remained remarkably uniform throughout the centuries.[39] When an inquisitor arrived in the locality he had been newly appointed to, his first act was to pronounce a sermon—with all due publicity—inviting the faithful to report to him any case, or even suspicions, of heresy. This call for delations opened a "time of grace," a short period of time during which also repentant heretics or their accomplices who turned themselves in would not have been condemned, but simply given spiritual penances and reconciled with the Church. Such a policy reflected clearly the double character of the tribunal, which was at the same time a judicial and a penitential institution, seeking to punish heretics but willing to favor their repentance and readmit them to the fold.

Once enough information had been acquired, the inquisitor proceeded to summon those who had been accused by either witnesses or "public fame," that is, rumors and gossip. If he thought that evidence was solid enough, he would open a "inquisitio specialis," that is, an investigation against a specific individual, possibly hearing other witnesses, and questioning the suspect as many times as he saw fit. Defendants could not be denied access to defense counsel if they asked for it, and the court had to appoint a public defender to those who lacked the means to pay a lawyer; inquisitors, however, could refuse to allow lawyers they disliked. A copy of all accusations could be supplied upon request to the defendants and their attorneys, but without the names of witnesses as a protection from possible retaliations by the family and friends of the accused. Cross-examination of witnesses was therefore impossible, but defendants could give the court a list of "mortal enemies," people whose testimonies were to be considered altogether unreliable because of a supposed virulent enmity.[40]

The main goal of the inquisitor was to have the accused confess to the charges, for a twofold reason. On the one hand, from a penitential point of view, only confession could open the way for a defendant's abjuration and readmission in the Church, and therefore save his or her soul. On the other hand, from a legal angle confession was really the sole full proof available in cases of heresy, sorcery and witchcraft, as the other one—two eyewitnesses of the crime—was practically impossible to obtain for such offences. Torture, therefore, could be, and was, applied to elicit a confession, but its use was possible only if enough partial proofs existed: for instance, when several credible witnesses independently and unanimously confirmed direct reports of a crime which the accused denied, or if he or she had contradicted him/herself in the course of different hearings or had tried to escape, thus leading the court to a strong presumption of guilt. Besides these requirements, several other protocols protected the culprit from indiscriminate torture: they limited the length of application of torments, forbade particularly cruel systems and the torturing of children and the elderly or sick, dictated that confessions made under torture were valid only if confirmed by defendants the next day without torture, and emphatically excluded the possibility of repeating torture, which was to be applied only once.[41] In practice, however, no real safeguard existed if an inquisitor—or a secular judge, for that matter—was determined to obtain a confession, since regulations always left a wide margin for the "discretion" of court officials. Sessions of torture could be prolonged depending on the inquisitor's judgment, and above all they could take place more than once also by resorting to a linguistic escamotage like the one suggested in the *Directorium Inquisitorum*, of considering the various sessions each as a "continuation" of the first one, rather than repetitions.[42]

By denying charges under torture a defendant could annul the partial proofs against him/her and avoid condemnation, although normally he or she would still be considered "lightly suspect" and let go with some penances to perform.[43] If, on the contrary, the inquisitor had obtained a full confession, the trial could come to its conclusion, usually a very public event—as opposed to the secretive nature of the trial—nowadays known by the term used in the Portuguese Inquisition: the auto-da-fé, or act of faith. Large throngs of the faithful would crowd a church chosen by the court, and there the condemned person would read out loud a formal recantation of the errors committed, followed by the inquisitor's proclamation of the sentence. Punishments could be fairly light if the accused was a first-time offender who had confessed and repented: usually a period of confinement in the defendant's locality, or, on the contrary, of exile from it. If the crimes had been particularly serious, public whipping could be decreed or a jail term, on paper for life but usually commuted to shorter periods. Interestingly, the convicted heretic's goods were normally confiscated, and a part of them went to the local Inquisition: this explains why it was not rare for inquisitors to be accused of having issued a guilty verdict out of greed.[44] In all cases penances were also given (fasting, prayers, etc.), including a sort of shaming ritual in which the offender would be obliged to stand at a church's door on several Sundays, wearing some type of distinctive garment and holding candles, thus reminding everyone both of his/her condition as a lapsed Christian and of the fate awaiting heretics.

However, if the accused refused to recant or was a second-time offender—an unrepentant heretic in the first case, a relapsed in the second—the standard procedure was to hand him or her over to local authorities. It was a sort of green light which the inquisitor, who technically did not mete out the capital sentence, gave temporal justice (the "secular arm") to proceed with the punishment for heresy established by local laws, that is, most usually death by burning (Fig. 12).[45] Cooperation of lay magistrates was therefore of paramount importance, not only at this point, but throughout the trial, since inquisitors did not have police forces at their disposal to jail suspects, nor executioners to apply torture—clergy could not do it. It is true that a big helping hand on this side came from lay confraternities associated with the Inquisition, normally bearing the name of "Society of the Holy Cross," whose members could assist the inquisitor in his duty in several ways, as for example guarding and escorting suspects and defendants.[46]

Papal Inquisitors and Witches: Fourteenth to Mid-sixteenth Century

A comprehensive reconstruction of the activity of the Inquisition and of its logic is virtually impossible for this early period, as on the one hand inquisitorial documents which have survived are very scarce until the beginning of the sixteenth century (and really until the central decades of it), on the other hand there was no central supervising authority to dictate a more or less uniform policy. It is, however, possible to try to chart the operations of some of the local courts by piecing together evidence from indirect sources with information from the few surviving trials, but the reader should remember that any conclusion on these bases can only be an approximation of historical reality.[47]

Since doctrinal errors were the primary target of inquisitors, the inclusion of magic—not necessarily considered a form of heresy—into their field of action required some time.[48] Already in the first decades of their existence inquisitors had demanded from the Holy See the authority to try magicians and sorcerers, but that had been granted only when it could be shown that specific cases involved manifest heresy (as in a Bull by Pope Alexander IV, 1258).[49] During the course of the following century, however, a pope particularly concerned with the practice of demonic magic, John XXII, called the inquisitors to give special attention to this crime, *de facto* widening the jurisdiction of the tribunal to include it, as established with a Bull in 1326.[50] The following year, in Florence, Franciscan inquisitors condemned to death for heresy the astrologer, physician and poet Francesco Stabili, better known as Cecco d'Ascoli, charged with attributing to the purely naturalistic power of the stars the course of human events and even the shape of religions. Although apparently Cecco was not accused of demonic magic (which he was rumored to practice), his trial did signal the concerns raised by the practice of the occult arts—such as astrology—and the willingness of inquisitors to punish harshly even well-established figures such as Cecco.[51]

The attack on sorcery and witchcraft entered a more intense phase in the last decades of the fourteenth century, during which the Inquisition tribunals of the Italian states gained momentum. It is in fact in 1370 in Modena that a woman called Benvenuta Benincasa, nicknamed "Mangialoca," is tried on charges of demonic magic, confesses and is sentenced to perform a series of penances, including the obligation to wear a garment with two yellow crosses: the symbol of heresy.[52] The transcripts of her trial show the readiness of the Inquisition to detect traces of the devil's presence behind folklore beliefs and practices previously tolerated—such as prayers to stars, typical of traditional techniques of love magic—while keeping a still rather lenient approach to these crimes. At the same time, it testifies to the widespread diffusion of books of ritual magic, or necromancy, to which even female practitioners such as Benvenuta could have access.

Between the 1380s and 1390s, a few trials conducted in Milan also show how inquisitors analyzed and classified popular traditions under the heading of diabolism. Two women, Sibillia Zanni and Pierina Bugatis, confessed to having attended nocturnal assemblies presided over by a mysterious beneficent female figure, variously referred to as "Madonna Oriente" or "Diana," who was paid homage to by her followers, taught them the magic arts and resurrected the animals eaten at the banquets held at the meetings. Their tales, reminiscent of pre-Christian fertility cults and rituals centered around female deities of abundance (such as the pagan goddess Diana), were quickly interpreted by judges as forms of devil-worship, in which Satan had presented himself under various guises to deceive incautious women; and both Sibillia and Pierina were eventually sentenced to death in 1390.[53]

One city in which the repression of magic and sorcery left significant traces in these years is Florence, where several men and women were executed or anyway punished with severity between the 1370s and the third decade of the fifteenth century. They came from all different social groups, and their deeds ranged from complex magical operations, such as invoking demons with formulas learned from books in order to foretell the future, to the most common techniques of love magic. In 1384 one Niccolò Consigli was burned at the stake for having practiced demonic magic, fumigating with incense and myrrh a wax image of a man in the name of the demons Lucifer, Satan, and Beelzebub in order to kill that man, among many other things. Giovanna, daughter of Francesco "El Toso," was convicted for her nefarious magic love operations—such as giving "a little of her menses" mixed with wine to the man she wanted to bind to herself—and beheaded in 1427.[54] Interestingly, however, we find no trace of those folkloric cults, best expressed in the Milanese trials of Sibillia and Pierina, which theologians were in the process of transforming into the witches' sabbat. These Florentine cases are significant also because they show how secular authorities were keen to strike at magicians and sorceresses: not only did they cooperate with the local inquisitor, but several times tried and condemned on their own Satan's alleged servants applying secular laws against heresy and municipal statutes which punished harmful magic.

The impression one gets from looking at the series of known witchcraft cases for a good part of the fifteenth century is, in fact, that secular authorities were much more active than inquisitors in the peninsula. It is true that such an impression could be simply the result of the paucity of documentation we mentioned; all available sources, though, do confirm the leading role taken by regular lay justice. This is the case with Matteuccia di Francesco, a woman burned at the stake in 1428 at Todi, in the central region of Umbria, by a municipal court. She was found guilty of having used an unguent made with fat from a vulture, blood of an owl and of suckling babies, to transform herself into a cat and to fly, riding on the devil in the shape of a goat, to the walnut tree of Benevento, one of the most famous meeting places for Italian witches.[55] Between the 1440s and 1450s other executions were decreed by secular courts in Perugia and Ferrara, and a significant witch-hunt took place in the Val Leventina.[56] Very likely, as the threat posed by earlier medieval heretical sects had faded, several Inquisition tribunals entered into a sort of lethargy, due also to a general decline of the discipline and organization of the Franciscan and Dominican friars, who were responsible for the operations.[57] In fact, whenever influential and popular personalities from these two orders put some effort into the repression of witchcraft, the results were remarkable, as with Bernardino of Siena's intense preaching campaign in Rome, which brought the burning of two sorceresses in 1426 (although it is not clear what court condemned them).[58]

Nevertheless, a sharp change in this trend is discernible starting from the last quarter of the fifteenth century, when inquisitors in the north of Italy began to launch mass trials, with dozens of people executed for witchcraft. This is the case of the Inquisition of Como (Lombardy), which burned at the stake about forty people around 1485 in the mountainous county of Bormio in the Valtellina, as we learn indirectly from repeated and admiring mentions in the *Malleus Maleficarum*.[59] The loss of the archives of the Inquisition in Como deprives us of information on a tribunal which was very likely one of the most active in the Italian peninsula throughout the first decades of the sixteenth century: other indirect but reliable sources mention about sixty people executed for witchcraft in that town during the year 1513 alone, while the important demonologist and inquisitor Bartolomeo Spina, writing around 1520, recounts that over the previous few years the Inquisition there had been trying on average one thousand witches per year, and of these more than one hundred had been burned at the stake, likewise each year.[60] These figures are exaggerated, as such a pace would exceed even the highest peaks of witch-hunting by the much better organized secular courts in the area of the Holy Roman Empire during the following century; but they are perhaps less far from reality than one might think. In fact, we find corroborating evidence in a passage by the jurist Alciato, whose influential skeptical opinions have been discussed previously. He mentions a massive witch-hunt with over one hundred women executed by the Inquisition around 1516, again in the Valtellina: the harshness of these persecutions, he relates, had sparked a violent unrest among the peasants, and the trials had been taken over by the local bishop, who called on Alciato for advice.[61]

Interestingly, in those same years another large-scale campaign against witches was taking place in the neighboring Val Camonica, a remote valley then under the Republic of Venice: in 1518 sixty-two people had been sentenced to death by both the bishop of Brescia and the inquisitor, while an unspecified but staggering number were awaiting trial.[62] According to local traditions, thousands of women and men from all over Italy would gather at the Tonale pass, at the head of the valley, in what Venetian officials and churchmen on site were quick to interpret as sabbats of huge proportions. However, the repressions in Val Camonica had exceeded any limit, and strong protests had erupted against the greed of inquisitors, as many people had been convicted only to extort their money. Repeated interventions from the top executive committees of the Venetian government, sharply critical of the Inquisition's policy, caused first a revision of the trials by new judges, and finally an end to the prosecutions altogether in 1521.

The Alpine areas, at present between Switzerland and the territories of the Italian regions of Lombardy and Trentino, were therefore at the center of witch-hunting in the Italian peninsula at the beginning of the sixteenth century, although even less mountainous and remote localities saw the outbreak of fairly large panics. This was the case of the rural village of Venegono Superiore, on the main road between Milan and Varese (Lombardy), where in 1520 seven women were consigned by the inquisitor of Milan to local authorities to be burned for having killed children and adults with spells and having participated in the sabbat.[63] Equally striking is the case of Mirandola, a prosperous town in the fertile Po Valley (today in the region of Emilia), the capital of a tiny principality where the inquisitor of Parma and Reggio sent at least ten people to the stake between 1522 and 1523.[64] The witch-hunt in Mirandola stands out also because of the role played in it by the local lord, Count Gianfrancesco Pico. Nephew to the famous Renaissance thinker Giovanni Pico della Mirandola and a prominent philosopher in his own right, Count Pico lent total support to the Inquisition, probably witnessed several trials out of curiosity, and eventually devoted an ambitious work—the dialogue *Strix* (1523)—to persuading the skeptics that witchcraft was a terrifying reality[65] (Fig. 11).

Given available information, there are solid grounds to conclude that a major escalation in the repression of witchcraft took place at the beginning of the sixteenth century. Perhaps the highest peak in the history of witch-hunting in the Italian states was reached between the second and the third decade of the century, at least as far as figures of capital sentences are concerned.[66] It is likewise possible to affirm that the areas most affected were all located north of the Apennines, with a particular concentration in the territories of the duchy of Milan and especially in the Alpine valleys. More tentatively, it can be affirmed that known witch-hunts seem distributed predominantly in rural, and especially mountainous, areas. On the contrary urban episodes, such as that of Mirandola, appear to have been isolated exceptions in the Italian peninsula; in Mirandola, furthermore, many of the accused came from the countryside, and contingent reasons—like the strong determination of Count Pico to punish the witches—probably had a decisive weight.

Besides large witch-panics such as those mentioned, which clearly required exceptional resources and very likely monopolized the energies of the relevant tribunals, the early sixteenth century seems characterized also by a widespread increase in the ordinary activity of inquisitors, that is, by numerous individual trials against single magicians or sorceresses. Such is the situation documented at Venice and Modena, two of the tribunals whose archives are best preserved, between the second decade of the century and the 1530s. The volume of prosecutions for charms of love magic, healing potions and remedies, and magical techniques to foretell the future, grows, in some cases sharply, under the leadership of particularly determined judges in these two cities.[67] For the most part, the cases documented have two features in common: an urban setting—either the people tried came from cities or towns, or their activity took place there, or (most often) both—and the generally mild punishments meted out by inquisitors, in sharp contrast with the harshness of the larger witch-hunts. No significant traces of belief in the pact with the devil or the sabbat are found in the records, with the remarkable exception of one woman, Orsolina Toni, nicknamed "La Rossa" ("the Red"), from the village of Sassorosso in the Apennines. La Rossa, tried in Modena in 1539, was tortured repeatedly and gave a standard confession of diabolical witchcraft, but received a relatively light sentence (public humiliation and house arrest).[68] By the time Orsolina's trial had come to a conclusion, however, another target was beginning to displace sorcerers and witches in the Italian inquisitors' purview: Italian Protestants.

The Roman Inquisition and Witchcraft: 1542-1600

The diffusion of Protestant doctrines in the Italian states, particularly north of the Apennines, began early. In the 1520s we already find trials against individuals generically defined as "Lutherans" by inquisitors.[69] As heterodox ideas spread quickly, creating well-rooted communities of believers (especially in urban centers), the Catholic hierarchy realized that the magnitude of the threat required a radical reorganization of the repressive apparatus. Thus in 1542 Pope Paul III instituted a special committee composed of six cardinals, in charge of overseeing the prosecution of heretics in the Italian peninsula.[70]

The new institution bore the name of Holy Office of the Inquisition, and is nowadays referred to interchangeably as either the Holy Office or the Roman Inquisition to distinguish it from the earlier Iberian versions it was modeled after, the Spanish and the Portuguese Inquisitions. Like its antecedents, its key feature was the centralization of functions, meaning that the six members of the committee had absolute control over the workings of local tribunals, from the appointment of judges to all the decisions of importance these had to take: when to torture a suspect, whether evidence was solid enough to condemn someone, what kind of punishment to inflict, and so on. Contacts with the various branches were kept through incessant correspondence, as local inquisitors systematically wrote to ask for advice or help, and the cardinals in Rome, besides responding to their queries, often required that copies of entire trials be supplied to them.

During the roughly forty years following its foundation in 1542, the Roman Inquisition, whose efficiency increased greatly under the pontificate of such hardliners as Paul IV (1555-59) and Pius V (1566-72), devoted its resources almost entirely to the persecution of Protestantism, and the local tribunals were to react accordingly. As a direct result, the repression of magic and witchcraft gradually shifted from constituting a priority of inquisitors in the field to becoming a merely residual function of their office: eighty percent of the cases tried by the Inquisition in Venice between 1547 and 1582 involved Italian Protestants, seventy-five percent in the Friuli area, on the mainland north-east of Venice.[71] Trials for sorcery and magic become very rare, with long periods of nearly complete neglect: in Modena, for example, during 1540-49 only four women were investigated on charges of magic out of a total of twenty-eight cases opened. In the following decades the average is about one case per year or less (seventeen between 1550 and 1565, only twelve during 1566-80 of a total of 110 and 155 cases, respectively), in marked contrast with the much more sustained pace of the earlier years (thirty-one cases in the period 1517-20 alone).[72]

After 1580, following the destruction of the Italian Protestant movement, witchcraft came back to occupy center stage, but in a context that was substantially different from that of the earlier decades of the century. Following the epoch-making Council of Trent (concluded in 1563), the Catholic Church launched an unprecedented campaign to control and change the religious practices and beliefs of the faithful, bringing them into line with new guidelines and standards. It was the beginning of the age of the Counter Reformation, or Catholic Reformation.[73] Henceforth, a particular emphasis was placed on fighting "superstitions," that is, the entire range of popular remedies and rituals meant to heal body and soul and to control feelings and events. The new approach stressed that all these practices were to be suspected of heresy even when they consisted of simple acts (the sign of the cross, lighting candles, etc.) or prayers licit in themselves, should these have been used for inappropriate and unauthorized purposes, or if their efficacy was based, in the eyes of the practitioner, on some form of magical effect. Under such circumstances demonic intervention was always presumed, and the practitioner had to be tried by the Inquisition.

Two decrees issued in 1586 and 1587 by a former inquisitor raised to the pontificate, Sixtus V, sanctioned this change, condemning a vast catalogue of popular superstitions previously regarded as harmless, many of which were based simply on unauthorized prayers and invocations to saints. The Holy Office was given the task of prosecuting such practices, and in consequence its jurisdiction greatly expanded at the expense of the bishops' courts, traditionally in charge of punishing "simple," non heretical, spells ("sortilegia simplicia").[74]

The new policy provoked an immediate increase of cases of magic and sorcery, which is discernible in the files of some local tribunals. In Venice, for example, defendants in cases of magical practices go from fifty-nine during 1547-85 to 319 between 1586 and 1630 (even though records are mostly lacking for the period 1593-1615). More generally, it can be noted that, while at the beginning of the 1580s sorcery represented one third of all cases dealt with by the Venetian version of the Inquisition, at the end of that same decade it made up one half, and this level was to be maintained until the middle of the seventeenth century.[75]

The Modenese tribunal follows a similar pattern, with eighty-eight cases of sorcery and magic brought before the court between 1581 and 1600, which exceeds the total of eighty cases over the entire previous period 1495-1580; as in Venice, in Modena the increase is particularly marked from 1600 onwards.[76] The change was not only quantitative, but also qualitative. On the one hand, we find many trials against simple folk healers, whose activity had never before been prosecuted so massively. On the other hand, we notice the gradual, virtual disappearance of trials for diabolical witchcraft. This latter aspect is all the more remarkable, since it appears at the same time as Sixtus V's decrees, which called for a stiffening of the Church's policy against *all* unorthodox practices.

While towards the end of the sixteenth century almost everywhere else in Europe witch-hunting was entering into its most intense phase, in the Italian peninsula the supreme board of the Roman Inquisition was adopting an increasingly cautious attitude towards witchcraft. As early as the 1570s it was clear that the cardinal-inquisitors considered the issue not a priority of the tribunal, but rather a potential source of trouble because easily conducive to mistakes and excesses which could backfire, stirring protests and opposition against the Holy Office.

Several of the not numerous witch-hunts of this period are the work of Cardinal Carlo Borromeo, archbishop of Milan and future saint. An immensely prestigious champion of Counter Reformation ideals whose zeal for reform was equaled only by a fanatical determination to exterminate the witches, Borromeo launched a witch-hunt in the Val Mesolcina (now in the Swiss canton of Grisons), which ended with the execution of ten people in 1583. Although too little is known of this episode, it is probable that the Holy Office's attitude in this case had been similar to that in 1569, when it had expressed—in vain—serious reservations against Borromeo's intention of sending to the stake four women from Lecco.[77]

In the last decades of the sixteenth century Borromeo was not alone, however, since secular governments and judges would sometimes take the lead in witchcraft prosecution. This is the case with the (superficially) well-known witch-craze in Triora, a hill town in the westernmost part of the Italian Riviera and an important outpost of the Republic of Genoa. After a first, unsuccessful attempt to exterminate local witches by a vicar of the Inquisition had resulted in the deaths of two imprisoned women (one killed by indiscriminate torture), the Genoese government sent a special commissar to Triora in 1588. Obsessively convinced of the presence of the devil's allies, Commissar Giulio Scribani submitted several women of the town to particularly long and brutal sessions of torture, causing the deaths of at least three of them. In the end, the main accused were transferred to the care of the inquisitor of Genoa, whose final decision on their fate remains unknown.[78]

Strong protests against the violation of the rules of due process in Triora had come, interestingly, from Cardinal Giulio Antonio Santoro, the head of the Holy Office. This is quite understandable in the context of a *de facto* disbelief in the reality of the sabbat, a viewpoint which recent research has found to have been adopted by the board of the Roman Inquisition from the end of the 1580s.[79] Supreme inquisitors began consistently ruling that the supposed witches' accusations did not give sufficient grounds to prosecute alleged accomplices, and thus blocked virtually all potential mass prosecutions. They insisted that the *corpus delicti*–proof of the connection between a harmful spell and the sickness or death of somebody—be present before prosecution could start. They systematically urged local courts to caution and respect of legal propriety in cases of witchcraft, stressing that more often than not the defendants–especially if women—were somewhat deluded and therefore not to be believed.

It is not easy to explain the reasons for the fairly quick adoption of such a cautious approach, especially as official statements on magic and related matters from several Counter Reformation popes—who chaired Holy Office's meetings—provided for harsher penalties for such offences. Interestingly, some of the new positions of the Holy Office echo opinions expressed by several opponents of the witch-hunts. This is the case with the old idea of the sabbat as a delusory experience of simpleminded women, found already in the canon *Episcopi*, which was reformulated and greatly expanded on by Alciato, Cardano, and above all Wier during the sixteenth century, as we have seen.[80] Furthermore, the prohibition to proceed on the basis of the witches' accusations alone had already been a key point in the works of lawyers Vignati and Ponzinibio, which had been violently rejected by Church officials over the previous decades.[81] It is as if some components of this cautious disbelief had gradually filtered through, reaching the higher levels of the Roman Inquisition especially via the works of skeptical jurists. Looking at witchcraft from this point of view could offer the Catholic hierarchy one major advantage: the possibility of defusing potentially large and disruptive witch-hunts by resorting mostly to legal arguments, applicable to specific situations without calling into question the general theological framework regarding the witches and their Master. At a time in which secular powers were increasingly resentful of the Church's interference in judicial matters (such as in the right of the Roman Inquisition to try individuals, overriding the jurisdiction of any other court), Roman cardinals must have seen witch-hunts as an unwelcome occasion for friction and conflicts with lay magistrates and governments, whose cooperation was needed to implement Counter Reformation measures.[82] In this context, a selectively skeptical approach, with strong foundations in the canon law tradition, was the best choice insofar as it permitted Church officials to save a façade of belief in the diabolical pact and the sabbat, while safely keeping their prosecution under control.

Already in the late 1570s some of the top advisors of the Holy Office had begun weaving legal cautions and safeguards into the fabric of inquisitorial literature, as in the new edition of Eymeric's *Directorium Inquisitorum* by the influential Aragonese jurist Francisco Peña (1578), whose extensive commentary represents one remarkable effort at conciliating the positions of the *Malleus Maleficarum* with the much more prudent guidelines followed by contemporary inquisitors.[83] Such a balanced attitude did not rule out the theoretical possibility of diabolical witchcraft, but it "simply" stressed that delusions were very frequent in this field, and that consequently courts should proceed with the utmost care and moderation.

Significantly, for a long time this policy lacked official sanction by Church documents of any sort; it is only in the second decade of the seventeenth century that one finds a clear formulation of such principles in the *Instructio pro Formandis Processibus in Causis Strigum, Sortilegiorum et Maleficiorum*, probably by a member of the Holy Office, Cardinal Desiderio Scaglia.[84] The new attitude was likely regarded as potentially controversial, and therefore confined for decades to the case-by-case decisions of the Roman Inquisition's top board. However, its early practical adoption had channeled away from witchcraft energies and resources which the local courts were able to concentrate on one of the real priorities, that is, the crusade to stamp out popular magical beliefs and practices.

By having the Roman Inquisition focus on such a campaign, the main objective of the Counter Reformation Church was to discourage recourse to magical help—be it the healer's or the diviner's—while, conversely, encouraging the faithful to resort to ecclesiastically sponsored remedies to face everyday needs.[85] A combination of repression and indoctrination now characterized the attitude of the Inquisition. Benedictions, prayers, exorcism, the use of holy water—in a word, the whole corpus of the Catholic sacramentals—administered by authorized clergy, were to replace the "superstitious" activities of sorceresses and wizards. In the pursuit of this goal, a variety of agents was deployed: parish priests, confessors and preachers had to instill the new teachings with the tools of persuasion, but they were to be accompanied by the Holy Office, a stronger arm to uproot—with some violence, if necessary—the old customs and habits from the minds of the Lord's sheep. Judges would explain to offenders how to tell licit and illicit practices apart, threatening to use tougher methods if the lesson was not well learned.

Harsher sentences, in fact, were meted out systematically in cases involving abuses of sacraments, which were particularly targeted, along with the practice of demonic magic, in the last two decades of the sixteenth century. The attitude of courts tended to be generally lenient, on the contrary, towards first-time offenders who had presented themselves spontaneously to admit their faults. For many of these, in truth, the decision had not been spontaneous, but due to their confessors' insistence. New guidelines issued by the Holy Office required that priests deny absolution to whoever had confessed heretical behavior or beliefs of any kind. In such cases, confessants had first to pay a visit to the local inquisitor, who would listen to a full confession complete with the names of any accomplices, and then send the person back with his approval to the confessor for the assignment of a penance, absolution and final readmission to regular Church practice.[86] Such integration of confession and Inquisition constituted a much more effective way of monitoring the faithful. Sunday sermons by increasingly better educated priests and more frequent confession made Catholic believers more and more aware of the line separating "right" from "wrong" thoughts or practices, as well as of the need to inform the confessor (and if necessary the inquisitor) of any violation. Guilty consciences became the Holy Office's best allies, pushing concerned faithful to report themselves and others in order to receive a benevolent treatment. The nature of the Inquisition had thus changed profoundly from that of the earlier times: it no longer aimed mainly at prosecuting single criminals through formal procedure, often inflicting tough punishments. Now its work came to follow more and more a penitential, rather than a judicial, logic, and sought to keep a very close eye on entire collectivities, favoring the intensity and the frequency of controls over severity.

This wider and improved network of controls accounts for the massive increase of trials we have pointed to earlier. There was also a qualitative change in the crimes prosecuted, insofar as there was a remarkable rise in the number of clergy tried for magical practices.[87] This was due mainly to the higher cultural and behavioral standards required from the lower clergy by Church authorities. Since parish priests and friars were now called upon to provide the faithful with correct alternatives to "superstitious" remedies, they were expected to know Catholic theology and liturgy enough to distinguish between licit and illicit uses of sacraments and sacramentals. However, the educational system instituted for the clergy by the Counter Reformation Church took many decades to become operative and effective, thus leaving several generations of priests with a lack of preparation not much different from that typical of the period prior to the Council of Trent. The tighter net used by the revamped Inquisition was now able to catch those many clergy who continued to see and use remedies of folkloric origin and ecclesiastical rites as if they were one and the same, very much like their parishioners, whose culture and traditions they fully shared. "Superstitious" priests and friars were among the many victims of the great design of the Counter Reformation Church, that of establishing complete control over the mental life of the population of Catholic Europe.

CHAPTER II

THE PRACTICE OF MAGIC: AN ITALIAN CITY DURING THE RENAISSANCE

Varieties of Magic

FOR CENTURIES, THE TRIBUNALS OF THE INQUISITION WATCHED OVER the thoughts and actions of the Italian populace—more or less attentively depending on the times and circumstances—to spot and punish those beliefs that were deemed to be in contrast with the dogmas and the teachings of the Catholic Church. As we have seen, most magical practices were regarded by inquisitors as at least potentially heretical, and therefore their users often interrogated, if not formally tried. Since recourse to magical help in the most diverse life situations was extremely widespread in pre-modern societies (such as those of the Italian states in the Renaissance period), inquisitors came to examine many sides of everyday experience normally of no interest for any other court: that is why Inquisition records highlight individual and collective attitudes towards illness, love, enmity, death, material or psychological emergencies of all kinds. Furthermore, as heresy could be insidiously hidden in gestures or words apparently harmless, or even confined to the realm of the mind, the task of the "tribunal of the faith" was to scrutinize in depth both deeds and intentions of defendants. Hence the fact that Inquisition trials yield an enormous amount of information on the private habits, inner feelings and thoughts of Renaissance Italians, quite often outside of the tribunal's specific scope. Some historians have referred to this situation pointing to the close proximity of the inquisitor's role to that of a present day anthropologist, collecting data on customs and mentality through systematic questioning. Although, in my opinion, differences greatly outnumber similarities, this parallel can give an idea of the unique character of Inquisition records for the study of early modern European societies. They are a source of information about aspects of life we could not have known about otherwise.[1]

The richness and variety of this type of document makes the task of selecting and classifying the magical works described a very difficult one. I have chosen what is perhaps the simplest structure, grouping practices on the basis of their goal: the four broad categories are love magic, magical healing, divination, and *maleficium* (or harmful magic), this last somewhat hard to distinguish from love spells because of their similarity.[2] However, the chapter opens with a discussion of three topics that do not fit into any single group, but cut across several. The first one is diabolical witchcraft, that really stands alone outside of this classification scheme due to both the all-important weight of diabolism in it —unlike most other Modenese magical practices—and its rarity in the records we examined. The second will be learned magic, or necromancy, its sources and the people who practiced it. Consisting of techniques primarily drawn from books, necromancy required a certain degree of literacy and therefore was different from the more "popular" type of magic which was known and available, by way of oral transmission, to a much wider pool of users. However, such distinctions should not overshadow the coexistence of, and interaction between, oral and written culture in the world of magic. On the one hand, magical techniques have always been highly syncretic, based on a chaotic accumulation and mixture of words, objects, symbols, and rituals that—regardless of their origin—seemed to provide the practitioner with supernatural powers. On the other hand, in the early modern era boundaries between elite and popular culture were vague and mobile, often crossed by communications and exchanges which make the task of distinguishing "learned" from "popular" components of magic a very futile one.[3]

The third introductory topic is the relationship between magic and Catholic rituals: this is an issue that cannot really be confined to just one section, since virtually all types of magic either mimicked or borrowed extensively from the corpus of the Church's liturgy, and clergy were accordingly involved in all kinds of magical activities.

This last remark leads to the question of the identity of those who practiced magic, and of their clientele, dealt with in the last section of this chapter: the task here will be to show how differences of cultural, social, and gender identity account for the sometimes very different types of techniques used—or asked for—while, on the other hand, they did not prevent contacts and cooperation between individuals of very diverse backgrounds.

Diabolical Witchcraft

Night-flying witches and their meetings with Satan at the sabbat figure pretty marginally in the documentation produced by the Inquisition in Modena during the late fifteenth and the sixteenth centuries. Only in a handful of cases do we find witches who confess feats matching the elaborate descriptions given by demonological literature, and apparently never did such confessions lead to the burning of a witch at the stake. This is the situation one finds also in the files of the Inquisition in

Venice, the other tribunal whose activity is best known during this time period, so that one historian has written that the image of the "Venetian witch" was very unlike that of the devil's servant one finds in the *Malleus Maleficarum*.[4]

Nevertheless, elements variously related to what has been defined as the "cumulative concept" of witchcraft—the pact with the devil, the sabbat, the flight of the witch—do appear in several instances in the Modenese records. We find one example in a 1499 trial against a certain Giovanna Palli, a woman accused of bewitching children (and then offering to cure them). Giovanna tells one of her customers that her teacher in the magical arts had been a woman nicknamed "la Padela," who at night went to the sabbat ("striacium") with other people in a field where they would eat turnips ("navones") until dawn, magically blinding a man who had tried to spy on them.[5] Such a peculiar version of the sabbat, in which the devil is nowhere to be seen and the witches' revelries amount to a meager vegetarian picnic, probably retains some features of the ancient, pre-Christian fertility cults that the theories of inquisitors had gradually transformed into diabolical rites.[6] The Modenese inquisitor, however, Gregorio of Modena, seems totally uninterested in these elements: unlike other judges, he did not try to corner the defendant into admitting that the quasi-harmless picnic had been in reality a meeting of Satan's servants—as hinted at by the witness's mention of "striacium"—and the case was dropped altogether.

Even more significant is a court record on another woman, Zilia or Giglia, who, together with her mother, was supposed to have taken part in the "cursus"—literally "running," or "course"—another local name for the sabbat. A witness interrogated in 1519 says that these meetings, where great banquets were attended by large numbers, were presided over by a female figure, the "Lady of the Course" ("Domina cursus," also referred to sometimes as "Domina ludi," the "Lady of the Game"), who had the power to resuscitate the oxen eaten by the participants.[7] In-depth research has shown that these details belong to an ancient and very widespread complex of Indo-European myths, typical of traditional hunting societies, which was still meaningful, as a myth of plenty and rebirth, to the popular strata of northern Italian cities and countryside in the Renaissance period.[8] Beliefs very similar to these are attested in the 1390 trials of two women who were sentenced to death by the inquisitor of Milan.[9] However, Bartolomeo Spina, a prominent Dominican theologian who was inquisitor of Modena at the time, unlike his Milanese colleague, judged that Zilia did not deserve such a harsh punishment, and closed the investigations immediately. But the encounter with the "Lady of the Course" left a significant trace in the book Spina published in 1523, *Quaestio de Strigibus* ("The Problem of the Witches"), where he identifies this female figure with the devil and explains the apparently miraculous resuscitation of the oxen as diabolical deceit.

The *Quaestio de Strigibus* was a very important text, since it supported the *Malleus Maleficarum*'s thesis on the reality of witchcraft—not yet solidly established in the Italian peninsula—while attacking the skeptical positions of the canon *Episcopi*. Spina's authoritativeness, and his determined and active leadership of Modena's Inquisition, account not only for the marked increase in the number of cases heard by the tribunal over the time period he was in charge (1518-20), but probably also for a shift in attitudes noticeable in the judges that followed his term, who seem readier to discern the signs of diabolical witchcraft in the deeds of Modenese sorceresses.[10] Although it is hard to draw conclusions on this issue—also because the Inquisition files contain no trials from 1524 to 1529 inclusive—it is only starting from the 1530s that one finds trials of women who confess to having been "witches" in the full sense of the word.[11]

This is the case of Orsolina Toni, nicknamed la Rossa, from the mountain village of Sassorosso in the Frignano area, tried in 1539.[12] Orsolina's trial was not initiated in town by the inquisitor, but in the mountains where she lived by a local delegate who tortured her with fire—a very unusual system for the Modenese tribunal—before handing her over to the inquisitor of Ferrara and Modena. After several other sessions of torture, she confessed to having killed numerous children by sucking their blood at night and to having gone to the sabbat riding the devil in the shape of a ram. Apart from the defilement of things sacred, sexual intercourse with the devil was the main feature of these diabolical gatherings according to Orsolina, who declared that the "extraordinary carnal pleasure" witches both male and female received from it was the main reason they kept going to the sabbat. The conclusion of her trial was recorded, with all its colorful details, in the city's chronicle written by the notary Tommasino de' Lancellotti. Held on a holiday—28 October, feast of the saints Simon and Jude—to permit popular participation, the auto-da-fè attracted to the Church of San Domenico an enormous crowd of Modenese people that wanted to see the witch and hear about her crimes. Despite the seriousness of the charges, the Modenese inquisitor Tommaso of Morbegno condemned her to house arrest "for life" (which meant parole after a few years) and

to various spiritual penances, thus showing that even full-fledged confessions of diabolical witchcraft did not necessarily push the local court
to extreme measures.[14]

The growing concern about the spread of Protestantism in Modena
made the witches' heresy move away from the forefront of inquisitorial action. It was only in 1564 that the tribunal found once again an
accomplice of the devil, Antonia Vignola. A woman from the rural village of Gombola who had lived in Modena for twenty years, Antonia
was accused of fairly common techniques of love magic and *maleficium*, but after a session of torture had started confessing the full range
of witchcraft crimes: at the sabbat ("cursus") together with other persons—whom she duly names to the inquisitor—she had renounced
baptism, defiled the eucharist and given herself to the devil body and
soul.[15] But what is more interesting in her trial is the intervention of
Camillo Campeggi, inquisitor general of Ferrara and Modena, a man
known for the ruthlessness with which he had repressed Protestant
beliefs: accepting Antonia's protests that her confessions had been
extorted with the threat of torture, Campeggi reopened the case and in
the end released her, thus overriding the (rather light) sentence previously issued by his vicar.[16]

It is therefore clear even from this quick survey that the nearly complete absence of cases of diabolical witchcraft in sixteenth century
Modena can be attributed to the combined effect of the timely insurgence of heterodox ideas—that directed the inquisitors away from the
witches at a moment ripe for the insurgence of witch-hunting—and of
the primarily urban focus of the Modenese tribunal. Likely, such a concentration of the Inquisition on the city was more of a necessity than a
deliberate choice, since the Inquisition long lacked resources and
organization to keep the vast rural and mountainous areas of the state
under control.[17] The inquisitors of Modena, therefore, dealt primarily
with beliefs and practices that did not have much in common with the
cumulative concept of witchcraft: it is perhaps no accident this latter is
found almost only in trials of women who came from the countryside
and the mountains. But practical reasons, valid as they may be in general, do not explain a certain reluctance of inquisitors to read in a diabolical key myths and rituals such as those found in the trials against
Palli, Zilia, and others. This attitude will be explained by examining, in
the next section, the peculiar theological approach to magic as a heresy,
an interpretation which characterized the policy of the Modenese tribunal along with those of many other Italian cities.

The lack of interest in diabolical witchcraft on the part of the Modenese inquisitors contrasts with a keen attention to all forms of magic which involved any type of dealing with the devil: in fact, the tribunal's records abound with cases of demonic magic.

Necromancy, as demonic magic was also called, was defined in antiquity as divination through consultation with the spirits of the dead, but in the middle ages it had acquired the quite different meaning of maleficent magical technique based on explicit conjurations of demons. Those who practiced it were believed, and believed themselves, to be able to summon these diabolical creatures and obtain from them whatever they asked. Since such an endeavor was considered both difficult and dangerous, it required highly structured rituals that had to be followed with absolute precision under pain of failure or even of serious risks for those who performed them. The complexity of these operations made necessary the recourse to written instructions, which since the centuries of the early middle ages constituted the biggest part of the books of necromancy, invaluable assets for any wizard since only access to them permitted the practice of this type of magic.[18]

Such texts were always highly heterogeneous, being a mixture of different cultural traditions, and very seldom could be attributed to a single, clearly identified author. Many of them had arrived in the Latin West during the twelfth and thirteenth centuries from Muslim Spain, whose intellectual elites represented for Christian Europe very important providers of Greek and Arab works of philosophy, astrology, alchemy, and magic throughout the middle ages. The books of such a provenance had a strong component relating to astrology: for example they instructed readers to perform certain rites at the moment corresponding to the appropriate celestial conjunction, or listed the names of the "spirits"—or else demons—presiding over the planets, which the magician could use to channel the energies coming from high above in the direction that served his purpose. Along with such "astral magic," as it is defined, other traditions shaped this genre, and especially techniques of various origin to conjure up demons, most often derived from Catholic exorcism rituals. The proximity of necromancy to exorcism is only one of the many points of contact, and confusion, between religion and magic in this time period.

Some of the necromancers' texts, such as the famous *Picatrix*, included a kind of philosophical framework that explained and justified the recourse to magical means to acquire superior knowledge of the mysteries of the universe; the great majority, however, were exclusively practical handbooks, filled with descriptions of magical recipes. The best known and more widely employed texts included *Liber Iuratus* (*The Sworn Book*), *Liber Centum Regum* (*Book of One Hundred Kings*), and especially *Clavicula Salomonis* (*The Key of Solomon*), the most famous in a long series of books of magic traditionally attributed to the ancient king of Israel, Solomon, who, according to the legend, had received from God power over demons.[19] Techniques described in such works consisted mainly of circles to be drawn on the ground (or also on parchment), invocations to summon demons, and sacrificial offerings both to entice and reward them.[20] Medieval and Renaissance wizards—and inquisitors—thought that through such means it was possible to obtain diabolical help and thus fulfill one's every wish: in most cases, that meant either acquiring knowledge about things secret—past, present and future—or influencing others' minds and wills.

Books of necromancy had been used by Modenese magicians as early as the fourteenth century, as proved in one of the earliest surviving trials, that against Benvenuta Mangialoca (1370), who recalls that her father-in-law Manfredino taught her how to invoke demons using "a big book," which allowed him to "perform marvelously horrible things."[21] The "golden age" of ritual magic, however, was reached in the sixteenth century, when a widespread circulation seemed to make such texts ubiquitous in town. Selections from the *Clavicula Salomonis* and another text of necromancy called *Angelica* were in the hands of Tommaso Seghizzi, an apothecary and barber-surgeon denounced in 1498,[22] as in those of several "magistri," or master-craftsmen (sometimes also meaning schoolteachers), and of many clergy, very often passionate practitioners of magical operations. Among these last a figure stands out, that of Don Guglielmo Campana, priest of the parish church of San Michele, who in 1517 confessed to the Inquisition the possession of a small library of six books such as the *Clavicula* and the *Almandel* (another work often attributed to King Solomon) as well as of several notebooks filled with recipes learned from other magicians.[23]

One of the most remarkable aspects of works of necromancy, in fact, was that they were always open texts, meaning that their owners participated actively in their (re)writing, adding to and modifying their contents according to their interests, preferences, and knowledge gained through experience. Most frequently handwritten—but sometimes collages of printed sheets and manuscript pages—such books were exchanged among, and copied by, magicians always eager to learn more powerful conjurations. Clearly, necromancy was practiced by persons who could read and write, but illiteracy was not an insuperable barrier, since contacts between magicians of vastly different backgrounds could provide an alternative path to written instructions. Besides the illiterate Benvenuta Mangialoca, instructed by her father-in-law, one remarkable example is that of another illiterate woman, the sorceress Anastasia nicknamed "la Frappona," whose trial in 1519 highlights her encounter with the humanist and poet Panfilo Sassi, also interested in the magical arts. From Sassi, Anastasia had learned how "to fumigate the spirit of love" according to the principles of necromancy, that is, to honor, through ritual fumigation, a demonic spirit supposed to create attraction between two people.[24] Furthermore, it was not rare to find texts of magic in apparently unlikely hands such as those of Bernardina Stadera, a woman denounced in 1499 for being a "charmer, conjurer and procuress," who read and copied invocations of demons from a document she had borrowed from some Servite friars and shared with her lover, the priest Antonio Montagnana.[25]

The attitude of the Modenese Inquisition toward demonic magic seems to reflect a very traditional theological framework—based on Aquinas' doctrine—such as that outlined in one the most widely used handbook for inquisitors, the *Directorium Inquisitorum* by Nicolau Eymeric. According to Eymeric, necromancers are guilty of heresy only if their practices have included some form—explicit or implicit— of worship, or at least veneration of or submission to, the devil or the demons: in this case, they are punishable as idolaters and apostates from the faith. Inquisitors had to examine attentively first of all the relationship between magicians and demons, to discover any sign of a cult alternative to Christianity; more subtly, they had to analyze also the quality of the intervention that a conjurer demanded from the demon. If this latter had been asked to force men or women to sin, or to foresee events which depended only on the free will of humans or God's decisions, then the magician was an idolater and therefore a heretic, since he (or she) had attributed to the devil—a creature—powers that belong solely to the Creator. If, on the contrary, the type of magic performed implied that the devil had been asked to do things which did not exceed the limits set by God—for example tempting humans to lustful deeds, or revealing events that occurred in distant places—then the performer was guilty simply of a mortal sin, not of heresy, and as such his deeds were not within the competence of the Inquisition.[26] In Eymeric's scheme, the magician is the conjurer of a demon over which he maintains some degree of control (though only apparent) through the rites of necromancy, while the witch, who participates in the sabbat, is not discussed. Therefore the pact with the evil spirit evoked is not the token of entry into Satan's sect, but only one possible form of the more general crime of "superstitio" ("superstition"), committed by human beings who—mistakenly—had thought that the devil could offer them miraculous powers and knowledge.

Such a very restrictive approach, which appears to have been only marginally influenced by the more recent demonology of the *Malleus Maleficarum*, did not substantially change over the entire century in Modena, and it goes a long way toward explaining not only why witch-hunts were rare events in the area, but also why condemnations for demonic magic were not frequent, either. Though often investigated, magicians were seldom found to have believed demons had powers, or deserved worship, which only God could and should have, and therefore their actions and thoughts were normally judged not to be heretical. This was especially the case with illiterate performers of magic, whose practices often involved conjurations of the "in the devil's name" type, but virtually never implied any conscious statement of the devil's preeminence over God.

Magic and Catholic Rituals

Perhaps the most striking feature of the trials of Modenese sorceresses and magicians is the omnipresence of elements, gestures, and words borrowed from Catholic liturgy. Furthermore, as it is rather uncommon to find techniques that do not have any connection to Church ritual, instances of the practice of the magic arts which do not involve in some capacity any Catholic clergy are just as infrequent. Such a situation, at first surprising, is actually quite understandable in the context of what English historian Keith Thomas has defined as the "magic of the medieval Church," referring to the fact that the idea of the Church as it was both proposed by hierarchies and perceived by the majority of the faithful was that of a storehouse of supernatural powers which could be used to provide divine protection for human life's many aspects.[27] Believers saw sacraments and sacramentals first and foremost as channels through which those powers deployed their efficacy: special benedictions ensured abundance of the year's crops, the fertility of the nuptial bed, or the recovery of the sick. Masses were said to drive away storms, or the drought, while exorcism protected against, or freed from, the assaults of the Evil one. No particular inner disposition was required from the faithful to cooperate with the Church's holy tools, as these were supposed to work unfailingly; no substantial difference existed, then, between magical practices and ecclesiastical rituals, since both were thought to have material, rather than spiritual, effects, and it was believed that tangible results would be automatically achieved if correct procedures were followed.[28]

It becomes clear now why so many charms and incantations resembled Catholic prayers or ceremonies, since they had incorporated wording and signs that seemed to contain the key to access wondrous powers. A complex relationship existed between magic and religion, which involved overlapping, integration and competition at the same time. Many magical practices functioned as an integration of the Church's sacramental system. If the nuptial rite bestowed God's blessing on a couple, love spells helped find a spouse, or fixed troubled marriages. Healing magic also was to some extent an expansion of Catholic rites such as the anointing of the sick, providing a set of remedies more articulate and better responsive to different situations. One could actually say that magic and religion did not really exist as two separate dimensions, but rather constituted together what one historian has called the "system of the sacred," meaning the set of the beliefs about, and the various means of gaining access to, the supernatural sphere.[29]

The system, however, was not limited to the beneficent side, but included the maleficent, diabolical one, as these were seen not as conflicting worlds, but as the two sides of the same coin. The same sacred powers that healed could also harm, they could spark love or, just as well, hate: priests blessed the sick in the name of God, and sorcerers provoked disease conjuring the devil through spells structured as prayers—or vice versa.

In fact, one remarkable consequence of the integration of the divine and the diabolical into one unified system was the systematic involvement—direct or indirect—of Catholic clergy in magical practices. Priests and friars perceived themselves, and were perceived, as the official mediators between the everyday world and the "sacred system," capable of putting superhuman powers to whatever use was needed. Partly due to the lower clergy's full immersion in the culture of its flock (owing to a lack of formal training and education which lasted well into the seventeenth century), the massive presence of wizard-priests in the Inquisition trials also reflects the lack of clear boundaries between licit and illicit uses of the Church's apparatus. Healers, sorceresses, and priests had at their disposal parallel sets of magical tools, in which correspondences, and also conflicts, abounded; correspondingly, all these figures could be called on by the population for roughly the same purposes, often entering into competition between them.[30]

Among the many sorcerer-priests that crowd Modenese Inquisition records, however, one appeared as definitely able to outdo any competitor, and often to outwit many of his clients: Don Guglielmo Campana, rector of the parish of San Michele and exorcist in the cathedral of Modena, whose career as a healer, conjurer of demons and treasure-finder spanned at least three decades by 1517, the year he was brought to trial. Campana's magical performances stand out among those of his peers because of their greater variety and their extremely syncretic features; they will thus figure prominently in this book, since they represent a truly unique example of the diversity of sources and tools which could make up the repertoire of a literate, lower-middle-class magician in the early modern period.

The attitude of the Catholic Church towards the appropriation of things sacred for magical uses was not very consistent or uniform. At least since the early fourteenth century, any abuse of sacraments and sacramentals for such purposes had been considered a strong hint of heresy, and therefore a crime under the jurisdiction of the Inquisition.[31] The struggle against such a widespread phenomenon, however, does not seem to have been the priority of tribunals until the late sixteenth century. As far as Modena is concerned, inquisitors showed only sporadic interest and moderate severity vis-à-vis the extremely frequent use of holy things by wizards and sorceresses. Cases in which verdicts explicitly singled out inappropriate manipulations of consecrated elements as worthy of punishment were not frequent at the beginning of the fifteen hundreds, and significantly did not involve clergy.[32]

Things were to change only in the scenario of the Counter Reformation, when a renewed zeal to shape and control the forms of devotion brought a number of abuses to center stage, and the number of prosecutions of such crimes increased sharply. In this later phase, though, the Inquisition's outlook was to see the use of sacred rituals and elements in magic not so much as signs of worship of the devil, but rather as an illegal appropriation of what belonged rightfully to the Church.[33]

Love Magic

In the majority of the cases dealt with by the Inquisition it is love magic that stands out as the main activity of enchantresses and wizards. It was normal for Renaissance Italians of all conditions, especially women but also men, to resort to magic to create or strengthen love ties, be it to satisfy lustful passions or to arrange a good marriage. Erotic spells were more frequently asked for by women, mainly because social and gender norms forbade them to openly take initiatives in the area of love and marriage. Men resorted to magic, too, although more frequently to obtain occasional favors from a mistress than eternal affection from a wife. Likely because of these very reasons love magicians were more often women, who had at their disposal a seemingly endless array of techniques of the most different types.

A clear example of the overlapping and integration of magical operations and Church rites is that of the long and complex prayers ("orazioni") which were widely used by sorceresses (not just in Modena, but all over Italy) to spark love, the more popular ones addressed to Saint Daniel and Saint Martha.[34] These prayers, like necromantic techniques, could be learned and spread by both oral transmission and printed versions, which became popular from the latter decades of the sixteenth century. The unofficial prayer of Saint Daniel was considered by Costanza Zaccaria, nicknamed "Barbetta," "the most powerful" love magic, capable of forcing her lover Filippo to travel many miles to rejoin her. It required that thirty-three candles be lit on thirty-three mornings (clearly a reference to Christ's supposed age at crucifixion), while Costanza invoked the name of Filippo "by the Passion of Christ, by the nails, by the slaps..." and so on, eventually nominating all the "mysteries of the Passion" as in an apparently normal, orthodox litany.[35] Less orthodox was the part in which Filippo was invoked "by the sun and by the moon and the stars and the elements," by various foods, by the masses celebrated in Rome by bishops and archbishops: a list of items that was clearly reminiscent of the format of mainstream prayers.[36] Again, adopting such format and wording meant, for the performer, tapping the limitless source of powers that the Church's rituals seemed to contain: even the sacred event of Christ's Passion could be used to create profane love between a man and a woman.

Such love magic "orazioni," however, could have stronger non-Christian connotations, as in the case of the "prayers to the stars."

These could vary, but usually included invocations to the moon and/or to stars variously referred to as "Diana," or "the most beautiful in the sky" or "the first to appear." The other feature common to all variants was the manner of the prayer's use: performers—always women—had to be naked, or at least to be on their bare knees, to recite it (Fig. 13). Some procedures could be even more peculiar. Anastasia la Frappona used to go naked onto her roof—presumably to feel closer to the heavenly powers—with loose hair, to wait for the rising of the "most beautiful" star and invoke it saying: "God save you, star," and asking "that the star send an arrow to the heart of the man she wanted to be loved by."[37] Giulia of Bologna prayed to a "star called Diana," or the moon: "God save you, holy new moon." She was condemned by the Inquisition to abjure "the detestable error of paganism [...] following which one honors, worships, and prays to, the stars and the planets," that is, idolatry.[38] Such prayers had their remote origin in pre-Christian rituals of propitiation of natural elements and forces, but they borrowed both format and vocabulary from Christian tradition, therefore mixing invocations to God and to the stars and planets, which the performers did not perceive as being incompatible, but rather components of the same system of the sacred.

The two sides of the system—the divine and the diabolical one—could be present in similar or very unequal proportions in any magical practice. When love magic was meant to be more aggressive, the diabolical component was more marked, and that connected to the saints or God correspondingly less prominent or nonexistent. Typical, from this point of view, is another technique used by many Modenese sorceresses and known as "the hammer" ("dare martello," or "to give the hammer" meant to put a strong love spell on someone). This technique—which had scores of variants—consisted in putting a horseshoe first in the fire, hitting it with a hammer while saying the following words: "I do not hit and hammer you, horseshoe, but rather the heart, the mind, the imagination, the feelings and the vigor of such-and-such," naming the spell's victim. The horseshoe was then put into a chamber pot filled with urine, saying: "It is not you that I let sizzle, horseshoe, but rather the mind, the heart, the vigor and feelings of such and such, until he/she will come to this house to do as I please."[39] The performer had to repeat this routine until the person was forced to come. What is interesting to stress here is, on the one hand, the importance of ritually listing the organs and faculties that the spell was supposed to harm (as if the intended effect could be reached more easily by enumerating them); on the other hand, the fact that every single act required by the operation, from buying the wood to lighting up the fire to hitting the horseshoe or throwing it in the pot, had to be done "in the name of the great devil."

The invocation to Satan seemed the natural, best guarantee to obtain, also through the infliction of pain, what he was recognized in the sacred system as presiding over: carnal love. This last aspect was particularly evident in another practice, resorted to by Giulia of Bologna, which also required that the devil be invoked at every step. She instructed a certain Margherita Zucconi to buy a rooster and put it into a pierced basket through which its head would stick out, so that the poor beast could see food placed nearby but could not eat it. Starved to death, the rooster was then burned to ashes, and these scattered on the person whose love was sought.[40] The logic behind this was that of transferal: the consumption that had killed the rooster was "distilled" and transferred, by means of the ashes, onto the human victim, so that it would provoke a similar effect and in the end force him or her, out of a near-deadly love sickness, to give in to the desires of whoever had worked such a spell.

Still within the field of love magic, but with a much less aggressive content (and no mention of the devil), one finds the use of a baptized magnet, one of the most popular magical tools used by Italian enchantresses. Clearly based on one of the most fundamental principles of magic, that of similarity (the effect resembles its cause), this technique aimed at creating, or recreating, attraction between a man and a woman through the mysterious power of the magnet. The latter, though, would achieve this goal only if it had been in some form "treated" ("conciata"), as magicians used to say, through Catholic ritual: it was necessary that a priest either celebrate a certain number of masses over it, or baptize it, or both. The magnet could be hidden by the magician in a baby's swaddling bands, so that the priest would unknowingly baptize it; more frequently, however, clergy would willingly participate in such operations. Giulia of Bologna, tried in 1518, could count on the help of her lover, the priest Don Geminiano Trenti, to baptize the magnet with water from seven baptismal fonts, and then to have seven masses said over it. Anastasia la Frappona recounted how another clergyman, Don Sebastiano Montano, had christened a magnet "Giulio," her lover's name, in a ceremony in which she had performed the role of godmother.[41] She had then used it to touch Giulio, sometimes in artful ways such as kissing him while keeping the magnet in her mouth.

Very often love spells were hidden in, or otherwise based on, various foods, so that they could best enter the victim's body and influence it from within. The effects of such charms could be truly remarkable, as in the case of a "placenta" (a kind of focaccia, or flat bread) with which a certain "Baila" (possibly a wet nurse, "balia" in Italian) from the village of Campogalliano had bewitched Jacopo Cantini. The records do not mention the ingredients, but dwell at length on the consequences: Jacopo started "loathing his wife and children, while on the contrary greatly loved Baila and followed her everywhere, although she was a most disgusting and stinking woman." This spell was accompanied by its twin, another focaccia that Baila managed to give Jacopo's wife to eat, obtaining a perfectly identical effect: "she started loathing him, to the point that, when she approached her husband, or he approached her, they seemed to each other to be unbearably stinking."[42] Obviously such bewitchments could have the important function of explaining, and often excusing, socially unacceptable relationships, such as that between the respectable citizen Jacopo and a woman like Baila, whose very bad reputation "about the honesty of her body" meant that public opinion held her to be a prostitute.

An even more striking case was that of Anastasia la Frappona, who, thanks to her powerful spells, had made the wealthy Annibale Valentini fall in love with her to the point of marrying her although she was "of humble status, bad reputation, poor, and a foreigner." Anastasia was accused of the murder through magic of her first husband as well as of Annibale's wife, due the suspicious simultaneity of the two spouses' deaths, which had conveniently left Anastasia and Valentini free.[43] She was also suspected of having tried to bewitch Annibale's son by giving him some of her menses in food or drink, so that he would like her —an attempt to win approval from her husband's family, obviously opposed to his new wife.[44] Blood, because of its apparent connection to passion, was one of the favorite ingredients of love magic, especially if menstrual, given its close association with sex. Other bodily fluids also appealed to magicians, as for example human milk, often used to prepare cakes or focaccie that were supposed to create, or more often recreate, love and harmony in a couple.[45] Likely based on the principle of similarity, the use of milk aimed at solving the difficulties experienced by a couple by transferring to their life the kind of union that tied a suckling baby to the nursing mother.

While the above mentioned magical works belong to the realm of traditional, popular magic, other techniques were drawn by Modenese literate magicians from books of necromancy: the most common ones were voodoo dolls and invocations of demons' names written on slips of parchment. The former were wax statuettes prepared with a special procedure, like the one made by Giovanni Tassoni: "using red wax— the same as that candles are made from—mixed with saffron, he made a statuette, stuck a pin in its heart, and wrote on its forehead three names of demons, and put it first in water, then on the fire, reciting some demonic conjuration." The goal was to obligate a certain Margherita Fogliani, wife of the notary Pietro Gian Paolo Machiavelli, to reciprocate Giovanni's love for her. Failure to win Margherita's favor did not discourage the young patrician, who then attempted the same with a rich and attractive widow, Bianca Morano, whose name he wrote on the three dolls he had prepared.[46] In both cases, Giovanni was very likely applying what he had learned from the *Clavicula Salomonis*: this book figured in the library of Don Guglielmo Campana, his teacher in the magical arts, and included detailed instructions on how to make dolls with beeswax, pierce them on the side of the heart, write on them with a stylus the names of demons such as "Sichel" and "Richel," put them in water and then on a fire of fragrant wood. The aim was to make the victim's life unbearable until he or she would give in to the performer's advances.[47]

It is noteworthy how close love and harmful magic could be: the pins and the fire, symbolizing here love's pains and the burning heat of passion, were used for *maleficium* as well, with only a difference in degree, as in this latter case the torments would have been used to bring about the death of the victim. Such operations—among the most universally practiced, in all times and places—are defined as "sympathetic magic," since they were supposed to work on the basis of the principle that any action performed on the image would have an effect on the victim's body and soul, too. The recourse to necromantic ritual added the intervention of the demons, who were supposed to carry out its effect. Significantly, the efficacy of the operation was based not only on demonic partnership, but also on Catholic ritual, since wax dolls were very often baptized—best if by a real priest—in the name of the victim, so that the identification of the person with his/her image could be complete. Antonio Capretti was a master in this art, which he had learned from one of his books of necromancy, and then eventually taught to Don Campana.[48]

Another technique featured "magical slips," that is, invocations to demons written on small pieces of paper or parchment, which had either to come in contact with the person who was the operation's target, or to be hidden in a place where the victim used to go often. Texts of necromancy supplied both names of demons and "characters," special signs thought to possess the power to conjure them and force them to obey. Interestingly, a very important component of such practices was the special type of medium for the slip. Magicians very often used what was known as "carta vergine" (literally "virgin paper"), meaning a kind of parchment made of lambskin (or kidskin), and prepared according to complicated procedures that mimicked those prescribed in the Catholic ritual for the benediction of objects and places. Such ceremonies were meant to purify a spell's components, enhancing its efficacy.

The mixing of the liturgical with the demonic could be even more pronounced, as found in the file opened in 1496 against the *magister* Pietro d'Arezzo, owner of books of necromancy, who had prepared a scrap of virgin parchment, on which several "diabolical characters" had been drawn along with the shape of a male organ.[49] His client, Ludovico Bottacci, who wanted to spark a woman's "unchaste love" toward himself, was instructed to attend mass holding the slip in his hand, and to participate in the rite answering negatively to the priest's formulas (e.g. when the priest said "May the Lord be with you," he was to reply "You're lying"). Likely such an operation was supposed to exploit and pervert the great power of the mass, transforming it from a source of spiritual salvation to one of carnal perdition.

Magical slips could be meant to work not only through diabolical help, but also thanks to the assistance of Christian holiness. Formulas based on figures or events drawn from Scriptures were written on pieces of paper, or parchment, or even on leaves. Don Campana used to give his clientele slips on which he had written sentences like "May peace be between such and such persons just as there was peace between Adam and Eve, Abraham and Sarah." Here such a formula, through the frequently used format "just as … so," was supposed to recreate between the client and his/her spouse the kind of concord that had reigned between the Old Testament's patriarchs and their wives.[50]

Divination

Partnership with the demons provided early modern magicians with one great opportunity to look into the future, or to discover facts that happened in secret or in far away places, through the powers that God had granted to the fallen angels. Catholic doctrine held that these supernatural beings possessed a supernatural intelligence and an incomparable experience of earthly affairs (due to their eternity), and were capable of both fantastic speed and invisibility. Thanks to these qualities they were thought to have an extraordinary (though not error-free) ability to foretell the course of human actions, and to know events or people's whereabouts as no one else could.[51]

Anyway, since demons were also supposed to be dangerous characters, often unwilling to share their information, magicians had to resort to tough means: that is why books of necromancy abound with descriptions of procedures to force demons to cooperate. Formulas to conjure spirits resembled very closely those used by Catholic priests in the rituals of exorcism. Indeed, conjurations were seen as functionally equivalent to exorcism as both had the objective to control demons, the "only" difference being that the former attempted to attract them while the latter to banish them.[52]

Necromancy's many points of contact with liturgy are best shown by one magical operation in particular, the hunt for hidden treasures. Based on the widespread belief in the possibility of countless such troves (not entirely without grounds, given the unavailability of banking services to the majority of pre-modern Europeans), searches for treasures were undertaken frequently by necromancers and a mostly upper-class clientele. The need for an expert of demonic magic in such enterprises was twofold: on the one hand, demons were considered to be a prime source of information on treasures' locations, and had to be interrogated about it; on the other hand, they were thought to stand guard over hidden riches, and therefore had to be dealt with in order for the hunt to be successful.[53] A deposition against a necromancer, Antonio Capretti, gives an idea of how frightening an experience a treasure hunt could be: Capretti had led a group of six or seven to Mount Valestro, near Reggio Emilia, where, in order to find the treasure, he had to perform a series of nine demonic invocations. But, as the inquisitor writes: "At the first invocation wind began to blow, and it got stronger and stronger at the following ones ... so that Antonio could not proceed to the ninth one since he had lost his strength, and after the sixth invocation came such a terrible wind and hailstorm, that the whole county was devastated for many miles around the mountain."[54]

If demons—through their ability to stir up awful tempests—could make a treasure hunt such a dangerous endeavor, the best way to keep them under control was to enroll the help of a priest, who could resort to exorcism. Don Guglielmo Campana was the most sought-after expert in this field. In a perfect integration of magical means with Christian liturgy, he used to exorcize a possessed person first to get information on where a treasure was hidden, then went to the place indicated and tried to locate the precise spot with divining rods on which he had written verses from the Roman Ritual and the Psalms.[55] Meanwhile, he celebrated masses asking God to help with the enterprise and to keep storms away.[56]

Besides the recourse to exorcism or similar rituals, the methods that magicians were supposed to follow to receive revelations from the demons generally required the use of reflecting surfaces, like mirrors, glass vases, or simply basins filled with water, in which the demons would show either themselves or an image of the person or event on which information was needed.[57] With such magical operations, known generically as "scrying," necromancers boasted their ability not only to evoke demons, but to enclose them permanently in mirrors or in glass vials, so as to have them always at their disposal. These methods had long been condemned: in 1398 the faculty of theology of the University of Paris had defined any attempt "by magic arts to include, coerce and bind demons in stones, rings, mirrors, images" a form of idolatry because based on some form of worship of the devil.[58] Magicians, however, were undeterred and in Modena (as elsewhere) continued to practice fortune-telling, often with the water surface of basins. Frequently demons would show themselves as venerable bearded men. Such was the appearance of the spirit evoked by Zuan delle Piatte, a wandering healer and sorcerer from the Trentino region, using conjurations drawn from one of his books of necromancy, and also of the "evil spirit, in the shape of a bearded man" Don Campana used to conjure with a handbasin to get unspecified "responses."[59]

The most sought-after type of demonic helper was the "spiritus familiaris," literally a "servant spirit," or "familiar demon," bound in a crystal ball. This sort of personal demon was, one could say, a fashionable accessory, something that could be found in the hands of important magicians, as for example those of the astrologer of Duke Ercole I d'Este, ruler of Ferrara and Modena.[60] However, the "servant spirit" was not rare even at less lofty levels, and the records of the Modenese Inquisition show several instances of its use on the part of operators who had access to texts of ritual magic. At the end of the fifteenth century Tommaso Seghizzi, the apothecary whose books of conjurations were mentioned earlier, claimed to have one spirit in a crystal, and he was in good company: it was rumored that even the suffragan bishop of Modena, Jacopo Sandri, had one.[61] Interestingly enough, a kind of competition existed between the bishop's demon and that of a local sorceress, Bernardina Stadera. When the bishop's glass ball was placed near to hers, the former became "totus turbidus" ("all cloudy"), perhaps as a sign of hostility. Most often the queries addressed to personal demons were linked to love and marriage, and came from a female clientele. Don Campana was much in demand by women anxious to know "whether their husbands or lovers still loved them," and convinced that the priest's spirit servant could answer their question.[62] Bernardina Stadera's demon, similarly, was asked by one Giovanna Mascarelli to give news of her husband—who was in far-away Genoa—and had answered laconically: "Something is wrong with your husband Gaspar: he has another woman."[63]

Leaving the demon in the sphere of (at least partially) literate magicians, several scrying techniques existed which belonged to the realm of folklore, and were used by a wider pool of practitioners. Perhaps the most well-known was called "l'anghistara," and utilized a pitcher (in old Italian "anghistara") or anyway a transparent bowl filled with water, in which a virgin boy or girl would look to see the images of the future or past events that the magician wanted to know. Here the power of suggestion, enhanced by the atmosphere in which the operation was carried out—a dark room lit only by one or two candles, often blessed—was to stimulate the child, whose purity and innocence were seen as facilitating contacts with the supernatural and helping prevent frauds.[64]

One formula was crucial to the success of the procedure, the so-called "prayer to the angel" that had to be recited by the child and which, with many variants, went more or less as follows: "Holy angel/ white angel/ for your sanctity/ for our virginity /let me see who did such and such /Holy angel/ black angel/ you for your sanctity /and I for my virginity / let me know who has done this and that."[65] Very often used to find the whereabouts of lost or stolen property, this operation drew on the power of the Catholic sacred, but with a significant ambiguity reflected by the double nature of the angel invoked: white and black, heavenly and infernal at the same time, this creature was seen as ambivalent as the energies stemming from the sacred system, which magicians could access for both beneficent and malevolent purposes. At the end of the sixteenth century this practice was among those popular divination methods condemned by the Counter Reformation Church as intolerable "superstitions." The 1586 Bull *Coeli et Terrae* issued by Pope Sixtus V explicitly rejected the prayer to the angel as a disguised form of devil-worship.[66]

Sometimes sorceresses would resort to prayers and peculiar rituals to get information on future events through some special channel. One example is that of Anastasia la Frappona, who—a witness told the inquisitor—at night in her room would light a blessed candle before the crucifix and would pray kneeling totally naked and with her hair loose, asking to know whether a certain man would marry a certain woman. She would eventually go to sleep and see "in a vision that man—for whom all this was done—in a large flowery meadow, where a dining table was prepared," and learn directly from him what she wanted to know.[67] The witness had not heard the words Anastasia had recited, but possibly her prayers had been similar to those uttered by Benvenuta Mangialoca, the earliest Modenese sorceress we know (1370), to discover who had cast a maleficent spell on a given person: she used to light blessed candles, and to say, "Let us pray, strengthened by beneficial precepts," and would then recite ten "Hail Marys" and ten "Our Fathers."[68] Like Anastasia, Benvenuta would eventually see in a dream the image of the man who was responsible for the *maleficium*. In such cases, prayers and sacred objects seemed to serve as a preparation for an onyric experience that would provide the answer to the inquiry. The evidence from these trials is too thin to draw bold comparisons, but it certainly points to the great importance of the dimension of dreams and self-induced visions in the interpretation of witchcraft.[69] It is worth stressing how the meadow and the dining table mentioned by Anastasia immediately make one think of the sabbat's feats, that witches would reach through a dream-like journey. Interestingly enough, however, these elements did not arouse the slightest interest in the inquisitor, who did not try and see whether they hinted at the presence of the Evil one.

Another very common type of fortune-telling, mostly applied to the erotic sphere, was the casting of beans. Sorceresses used to have two (or more) broad beans "baptized," then would bite them, shake them in their hands together with pieces of alum, bread, blessed wax or other things, and then throw them in the air. They would then interpret the pattern formed by the fallen objects so as to understand whether love and attraction still reigned, or were going to start off, between two persons, or not. The rationale at work was probably that of analogy, based in this case on spatial relations: if the two beans fell close to one another, it meant sentimental closeness between man and woman.[70] Costanza Zaccaria anyway, through bean-casting was able not only to discover whether her spells had worked, but also to foretell to anxious women in love the arrival of their lovers.[71]

Maleficium

Modenese sorcery was not frequently aimed at provoking pain or illness for purely maleficent purposes. Harmful magic was mostly part of a wider strategy, which was meant to inflict pain only to bend more easily the will of the victim, and normally force him or her to surrender to the love of the person at whose request the spell had been cast.

One does find, nevertheless, instances in which magic was used—or was thought to have been used—with the intention of crippling or killing. Wasting diseases, that seemed to "dry up" the ailing person, were very often attributed to unnatural causes, namely to *maleficium*. Understanding *what* had caused somebody to fall sick, however, required ascertaining *why* disease had broken out in the first place. In traditional societies like those of pre-modern Italy, in fact, illness was seldom seen as a random event, but rather as a consequence of intentional ill-will, and a crucial condition for any cure to work was to find out who had been wishing harm to the victim. Parents and relatives of the patient would search for an explanation for a mysterious illness or wasting disease, tracing the cause of the malady to some kind of quarrel or grudge between the family of the bewitched and any individual known in the community as a charmer or sorceress.[72] Margherita Pazzani, a woman who had been kept in bed by a disease for three years, was convinced that Chiara Signorini and her husband Bartolomeo were responsible for her condition. Three years before, as a witness related to the inquisitor, Margherita had driven them out of a certain property of hers that the two farmed, and Chiara had publicly cursed her, "Cursed be Madonna [Lady] Margherita Pazzana and those from her family who kicked me out of this property, may they never have peace nor rest."[73]

Margherita had no doubts as to who was to blame for her sickness, but when things were not so clear families would seek the help of a witch-doctor, or folk healer, who could at the same time treat the disease and identify its cause, or responsible agent. The powers that a healer could use, however, were perceived as ambivalent: in the logic of the system of the sacred, these could be beneficent or also maleficent, depending on the methods and the intentions, and it was normally believed that "he who knows how to heal, knows also how to harm" ("qui scit sanare scit destruere").[74] That is why the person suspected of being responsible for somebody's condition was typically the same that was called to cure him/her, also because, in the general opinion, nobody else could know better what the problem was. Chiara Signorini was therefore a natural choice for the bed-ridden Margherita, who had promised to give her once again a property to farm and some supplies and cattle, in exchange for healing her in twenty days' time. But witches were known to have a bad temper, and to take offence at the slightest sign of disrespect or lack of consideration from their neighbors.[75] So Chiara stopped curing Margherita at the first hint that the agreement was disregarded. In the same fashion Giulia of Bologna had suspended treatment of the bewitched child of Giuliana Tosetti, and when the woman had asked her why, Giulia's angry reply had been: "Because you never called me again."[76] It was normally at this point that a patient's family, disappointed and discouraged, turned to outside authorities for retribution, and denounced the healer-sorcerer to the judge or the inquisitor.

Most often, it was the illness, and sometimes death, of newborns and children, to be blamed on sorcery. The context in which suspicions arose was one of widespread anxiety over the fate of sick babies, due to the extremely high infant mortality rates of that age. We see the effect of bad reputation at work in a 1520 trial against a woman from the country district of Castelvetro, known just as "la Menigotta." She was feared in the whole area for being "a witch and a sorceress," to the point that everybody would give her "everything she wants so that she will not have any reason to harm," and when she walked in the street "everybody got out of her way and hid their children." Yet this most frightening woman had once "resurrected a child, that had been judged dead by everyone, with a thousand superstitions, sucking every single joint of the child's body ... so that in the end he started to say: 'Alas, stop it!'"[77] This is a striking document on the perceived duplicity of a witch's role: feared because of her terrible harmful powers, but capable of an astonishing beneficent deed such as the raising of the dead. Interestingly enough, however, even la Menigotta's apparent miracle could be viewed with suspicion—and the miracle-worker reported to the Inquisition—since it resembled too closely the way night-flying witches were supposed to bewitch children, that is by sucking blood from their hands and feet.[78] Very probably this woman's exceptionally bad reputation—based on a well-known record of bewitchments—could throw an overwhelmingly negative light on anything she would do.

La Menigotta's way of treating an ailment is also typical of the way harmful magic was often supposed to work, that is, not so much by way of rituals or formulas, but rather through some kind of protracted, intense or anyway intentional contact—bodily or also just visual—with the victim. In the case of children, the contact could have taken the appearance of the most innocent act: for example, Giulia of Bologna had such a negative reputation in town as a witch, that a Giovan Pietro de Coperti could suspect her of having bewitched his nephew simply because she had once taken him in her arms, and he had been sick ever since.[79] These individuals were perceived as possessing an inherent ability to harm that would exude from their very beings without any need of special words or procedures. For example, Anastasia la Frappona was accused of having bewitched Ippolito Facchini simply by "rubbing her hand on Ippolito's back."[80] It was widely believed that witches could harm their victims just by staring fixedly at them, through the power of the "evil eye" ("malocchio," in Italian).[81] Giacoma di Bagarini was denounced in 1519 for having bewitched several children, whom she was then called upon to cure. Witnesses testified to having seen, during mass, Giacoma keep her gaze fixed on Andriola, son of Eleonora wife of Michele Antonio, and the boy's illness had followed the episode.[82]

There were, however, specific rituals to harm, and the trial of Chiara Signorini provides us with one remarkable example, when a witness relates the way Margherita Pazzani had been bewitched: Chiara, together with her whole family, had kneeled, and holding a candle she had prayed saying these words, "May the life of Chiara melt away just as this candle melts."[83] This *maleficium*, performed as if it were a normal devotional practice, underlines once more the fundamental ambivalence of the system of the sacred, in which prayers could be said either to heal or to bewitch, depending on the circumstances and the goals pursued by the witch/healer. The duplicity of means and scopes is apparent also in other magical techniques, which could be used to cause indifferently sickness or love-sickness. One conjuration used by Chiara, that of the "five devils," is a case in point: "Five fingers I place on the wall (on the ground)/ five devils I conjure/ nine drops of blood they draw from her/ six they give to me, three they keep for their labors/ and may she never have peace nor rest/ nor sleep nor good health/ and may not be able to lie nor move nor work in the fields/ until she will come to speak to me."[84] Here the goal was to make Margherita's health problems worsen by symbolically having the devil "draw blood" from her, until she changed her attitude towards Chiara. Significantly the same conjuration was used by Costanza Zaccaria— and by countless other sorceresses—to provoke or increase the pains of love of the man or woman desired.[85]

The intervention of the devil, often requested by lower-class witches, was suspected especially when symptoms of a supposed bewitchment seemed very similar to those of a demonic possession. In such cases a person would feel an alien presence move inside his or her body, causing the sense of pain to shift from one organ or limb to another, and sometimes would show even more typical signs, like speaking with alien voices. Now, possession and witchcraft were two different concepts. Witches were only rarely judged to be possessed by the devil, with whom they had willingly made a pact; conversely, those who were possessed were not necessarily thought to be responsible for it nor to have entered any formal agreement with the devil.[86] Yet there was a point of contact, the importance of which was increasingly emphasized in the course of the sixteenth century, namely the possibility that sorcerers and witches send the devil to torment their victims. It was believed that spells and other magical works could function as signals, indicating to the devil the target of the *maleficium*.[87]

Such operations were best carried out by operators who had familiarity with the infernal creatures, especially necromancers. It is therefore only natural to find Don Guglielmo Campana, well-known for his dealings with demons, to be the chief suspect in a series of bewitchments whose duration in time and resistance to any treatment indicated the likely presence of the Evil one. In the 1517 trial against the Modenese priest, two women in particular claimed to be vexed by demonic presences because of Don Guglielmo's operations: Caterina Maroverti and Lucrezia Pasini, whose illnesses went back many years in time and showed some of the symptoms mentioned above.

In Modena, there was a natural way of dealing with such problems: the recourse to the power of the patron Saint Geminiano, a great exorcist during his lifetime (in the fourth century), buried in the town's cathedral (Figs. 15 and 16). His tomb—known as the "ark"—located in the crypt of the church was renowned well beyond Modena as one of the best places to take possessed people in order to have them delivered, and a priest was especially appointed to this task as "exorcist of Saint Geminiano."[88] Exorcism, however, was not foolproof, and as a matter of fact had not succeeded with the two women, although it had brought to light the reasons of this failure. The demon that vexed Lucrezia, speaking next to Saint Geminiano's ark in a voice very different from the woman's, had openly accused Don Guglielmo: "I pray the power of God, Saint Geminiano and Saint Vincent that they be witnesses that it is you [i.e. Don Guglielmo] who keep me here," meaning inside the woman's body.[89] The demon itself—who was disclosed to be Astaroth, a top-ranking member of the infernal hierarchy—eventually explained that Don Guglielmo had conjured a devil in a wax doll he had made in the image of Lucrezia, thus provoking the demonic possession of the woman.[90] Even Modena's patron saint was powerless in such cases, but especially on this particular occasion, since the *maleficium* had been worked precisely by the exorcist of the cathedral of San Geminiano, who was no one else but the same Don Guglielmo. Exactly like any other healer, Don Campana was perceived as an ambivalent being: he could cure, expelling evil presences through exorcism, but he could just as well cause illness by calling demons to invade people's bodies, thus drawing on the darker side of his powers.[91] Granted, in his case the mixture of the divine and the demonic, of beneficial and harmful faculties had reached extreme levels, also because of Campana's double role of active necromancer and cathedral exorcist. All clergy, however, shared a similar position at the crossing of different fields, and behaved and were regarded as manipulators of ethically neutral powers, which could be turned to either evil or good purposes depending on the needs and the situations.

Magical Healing

Diseases were dealt with through magical techniques as frequently as love- and marriage-related problems. From the Inquisition's trials we receive the impression of a widespread recourse to healers—more commonly female but often male—who were more accessible in terms of culture and honorarium to a lower-class clientele than a regular physician. Their methods typically included traditional remedies based on the curative properties of plants, animal parts and other substances, used in conjunction with formulas and rituals that—very much like those of sorceresses and fortune-tellers—were a mixture of the religious and the magical. Traditional medicine, however, was not the only option available to patients and their families in Renaissance times, since at least two other possibilities existed: official medicine, and Church-sponsored remedies. The first one, of classical origin, based on the doctrine of the four humors and of their balance, was taught in the universities and practiced by licensed physicians and other health workers (for example barber-surgeons) who, under the physicians' supervision, would materially operate on sick bodies.[92] The Catholic Church, which accepted in part the theoretical framework of academic medicine, stressed anyway the medical efficacy of its own means, namely sacraments and sacramentals, to bring about a patient's recovery. Prayers and rituals, ecclesiastical authorities claimed, would produce not only spiritual, but also material benefits, actively contrasting disease and restoring the faithful's health.[93]

These three traditions did not exist and work as entirely separate worlds. First of all, sick people normally resorted to more than one healing method—especially when they did not obtain satisfactory results from the first attempt—and did not see them as incompatible. Historians refer to this situation as "medical pluralism," meaning both the variety of options available and the general willingness to try them all.[94] Secondly, communication between the different systems enabled frequent exchanges and a mixing of recipes and procedures. Some of these contacts are more obvious, as those between folk healers and clergy. On the one hand, lay practitioners regarded Church remedies as endowed with supernatural energies, and therefore incorporated wording and gestures of the Catholic ritual in their operations. On the other hand, lower clergy shared the same culture and vocabulary with the healers, and often creatively mixed sacramentals with magical healing techniques of popular origin.[95] Less obviously, during the Renaissance physicians were open, to some extent, to the lore and recipes of "wise women" and cunning folk, as some of them had a track of medical successes. Furthermore, distinction between the magical and the medical remained vague even at the level of academic medicine, and many official medical texts recommended cures based on a mix of natural components and written or recited formulas.[96]

A similar confusion blurred the difference between disease and bewitchment, as it was widely believed that the devil could cause virtually any ailment.[97] The language used in the witchcraft trials reveals a conception of illness as an attack carried out by an evil entity, which takes hold of a person's body. For example, a certain Caterina of Reno, declared her servant to the inquisitor in 1517, had been "detained" ("detencta") by disease for five years, and she was thought to be "sick or else bewitched."[98] Correspondingly, "to heal" and "to release" were interchangeable terms to indicate the task of healers and at the same time—significantly—that of exorcists. Demonic possession, the literal seizing of a person's body by the devil, was the paradigm of any illness, and it was therefore only natural that the means of Catholic ritual, and Catholic clergy, would be massively used and called upon by patients and their relatives.[99]

In fact, one of the simplest and most common healing techniques was the sign of the cross—a sacramental—made by a priest or by a lay healer over the patient's body, or better still, the sick organ or limb. So common was this gesture that the term "segnare" (to make the sign of the cross over someone or something) was used as a synonym for "curare" (to cure).[100] We see the systematic use of such signing in a 1531 trial against a semi-professional healer, one Brighento Brighenti from the rural village of Maranello who many years before had received some informal medical training from a physician. A certain Maddalena Ferrari related how she had been "dried up like a piece of wood" by a disease that official medicine could not cure, to the point that one physician had advised her to go seek the help of a sorcerer "so that maybe she could be released." When she had asked Brighento to take care of her condition, he had made the sign of the cross over her many times, on specific days and times and having a certain number of candles lit, in the end bringing about her recovery.[101]

Although in principle signing, due to its simplicity, could be practiced by anybody, only certain people could truly heal through it: they were thought to have "a good hand," an inborn ability which made some hands more apt and powerful than others at treating illnesses.[102] Especially when it was practiced by lay healers, signing was accompanied by narrative charms or *historiole*, that had the function of prayers and which almost always drew on the life of Christ, the Virgin Mary or the saints.[103] One example of signing from the trial of Brighento shows also an interesting combination of faith in the healing power of Christianity and anti-Semitism: "When Jesus Christ ascended to heaven/ Heaven and earth were shaken/ He met the Jewish dogs/ And they said, 'I am not shaking nor can I shake; I have on me *la carne crevata*'[hernia] / (Jesus) said: 'Blessed be he who will believe me/ He will never have *carne crevata*'/ In the name of the Father, the Son and the Holy Ghost."[104] The belief was that the recitation of such charms, accompanied by the sign of the cross, would transport the disease and the patient's suffering to a meta-historical level—that of divine powers (Christ)—where they would be eliminated.[105] Simpler was the charm used by Don Campana to cure toothache: he would sign the aching tooth with a knife, reciting the formula: "May the pain of this tooth be as sweet as the milk that the glorious Virgin Mary gave to Our Lord Jesus Christ."[106] Directing the point of a knife at the sick limb was a way of symbolically attacking the disease, and it was part of a whole series of remedies based on the "magic of points," whose efficacy was attested also by famous Renaissance physicians.[107]

In the 1519 trial against Giulia of Bologna we see how the cross, the power of herbs and special formulas could be used together. To diagnose whether the sick son of Giuliana Tosetti was bewitched, Giulia washed him with water in which she had previously boiled some fennel, whispering some words so that she could not be heard by her client. Then she poured that water in a basin and put it under the child's cradle, leaving a wooden cross to float in it for two hours. She finally inspected the basin and, seeing that the water had not congealed, concluded that the boy was not bewitched.[108] Fennel, referred to in Modena as the "good herb" ("erba bona") was believed to have strong anti-maleficent power, and was frequently used to counteract the power of evil spells.[109] Other herbs which had a similar reputation included rue, sage, alfalfa, and anethum. A certain Vincenzo of Reggio burned them to fumigate sick children, then threw the ashes in a stream, believing that, "just as the ashes flowed away, so a little later would the children's illness."[110] Here the running water was thought to symbolically carry away the disease along with the ashes, in a typical example of sympathetic magic.[111]

The properties of plants were always perceived to be partly natural and partly magical, and it was thought that performing specific rituals at particular moments could enhance their efficacy. Especially significant was the belief according to which the night on the eve of St. John the Baptist day, June 24 (Midsummer's Eve), had a truly special, supernatural status and therefore was the best time to perform a number of magical operations, including the picking of herbs to be used for healing purposes.[112] Certainly heir to some pre-Christian fertility festival celebrating the summer solstice, St. John's night was considered almost universally in pre-modern Europe a unique moment, which bestowed upon nature and humans extraordinary gifts: it was thought that the dew of that night not only cured illnesses, but made plants and other ingredients more powerful healers or charmers. On this night Costanza

Zaccaria used to pick the beans which served for her fortune-telling experiments, and also the herbs she mixed with flour in a focaccia she then fed to her lover to strengthen their relationship.[113] Don Guglielmo Campana also went on that night, with fellow wizards and accomplices, to gather the "seeds of fern," which he would give to children suffering from epilepsy ("mal caduco," or the "falling sickness," in old Italian). As ferns do not bear seeds, this was an actually impossible task, although magicians often attempted it. Legend had it that whoever had managed to see the flowering of ferns in the fleeting moment it took place (on St. John's night), and collected their seeds, could obtain from others whatever they wanted, for the seeds made them irresistible. The whole operation, however, was difficult and dangerous, since it was believed that demonic presences guarded the ferns at this delicate moment. Specific procedures had therefore to be followed, such as gathering the seeds with paper sheets bearing quotes from the Gospels, as Campana had prudently done. It is interesting to remark that, while he had attempted to justify himself by declaring that the seeds served a medical purpose, the inquisitor wrote that the priest had used them in reality to "win favor," thus rejecting Campana's exculpation and implicitly demonstrating his knowledge of the traditions connected to St. John's night.[114]

Don Guglielmo, however, did treat epilepsy, if not with fern certainly with other medicines. By his own confession, he gave to epileptic children powder of coral and peony to drink, while to adults he also gave powder of human cranium in broth. For both children and grown-ups he coupled naturalistic cures with prayers, candles and signs of the cross. Coral, peony, and human bones were accepted by official medicine as remedies for epilepsy and other illnesses, and recorded in authoritative treatises which recognized their efficacy albeit stressing that it had occult and quasi-magical causes.[115]

Campana's type of access to such sources, as well as the priest's vision of his own healing method, is disclosed in a revealing statement he made during his trial. After describing how he used to diagnose possible bewitchments by measuring the sick person's waist before and after the recitation of some prayer—a system commonly used by folk healers[116]—he added that, "to people bewitched he used to give also certain medicines, but before giving them he always sought the advice of a doctor or of an apothecary" ("medicum seu aromatarium").[117] Contacts with medical professionals seemed to Campana a good way to integrate the array of magico-religious remedies he normally deployed to treat sick people, and he saw no incompatibility between these two dimensions. Many other clergy who, like him, cured diseases with a combination of ecclesiastical and folkloric "superstitious" remedies, became eventually one of the main targets of the revamped Inquisition at the end of the sixteenth century. Don Guglielmo's case is highly significant of the multifaceted reality of medical pluralism reigning in the early modern period: priests, cunning men, sorceresses, and doctors shared bits of a worldview in which natural ingredients had or could acquire occult powers, and religious rituals and magical formulas could together expel evil forces from human bodies, thus reestablishing a person's health.

Magicians and Sorceresses: Who Were They?

Even a quick glance at the Modenese Inquisition files against witches and wizards shows that undisputedly witches in the town and its district were almost always women: of the 166 people tried or denounced for offences of magic and witchcraft during 1495-1600, 124 were women, while the remaining forty-two were men.[118] In other terms, women outnumbered men by three to one, representing seventy-five percent of all cases of sorcery, a proportion perfectly in line with the general European trend. Going beyond this first consideration, however, is not as easy, since Inquisition documents do not frequently mention the status or occupation of the women involved.

The impression is that, not surprisingly, sorceresses came mostly from the lower rungs of society, and that many of them were not married—either spinsters or widows. A strong hint pointing in this direction is the high frequency of prostitutes among the witches of Modena, one of the cases in which Inquisition records are generally explicit on the profession of the accused. Resorting to magic, especially to love spells, was a way for "public women" to try and keep their clientele loyal, or often to win the love of one—especially if wealthy—customer. This is a situation already documented at the beginning of the century, as some of the most sought-after sorceresses such as Bernardina Stadera, Anastasia la Frappona, Baila of Campogalliano, and others still, were known either to be positively involved in prostitution or at least to be women of "dishonorable life" (several lived in concubinage, some—interestingly—with priests). This trend increased very sharply after 1598, when the transferal of the capital city of the

Este duchy from Ferrara to Modena brought to town the many prostitutes that thrived on the ducal court's life: the heightened attention of the Inquisition to the breaching of moral codes, together with the authorities' conviction that prostitutes were particularly disposed to magical practices, account for the steep jump in the numbers of prosecuted women.[119]

It is relatively easy, on the contrary, to get an idea of who the Modenese men were that participated in magic and sorcery, since a good number of them were clergy. Such prevalence of ecclesiastics, whose reasons have been highlighted in our discussion on the system of the sacred, becomes apparent from the 1580s, while for earlier decades only a thorough analysis of all files (including those in which priests were not the main accused) reveals a likewise massive participation of priests and friars in magical practices. Over the period 1495-1523, for example, we can identify twenty clergy as having been involved while the documents mention many more without giving their names. However, only one priest was tried, and another one denounced, out of a total of ten men investigated by the Inquisition on charges of magic over the period mentioned. Figures of prosecuted clergy rise during 1580-1600, with twelve priests or friars out of a total of twenty-seven cases involving men.[120] Such a remarkable change, which brings clergy from twenty to forty-five percent of all men investigated, is certainly due to the reorganization of the Inquisition and to the refocusing of its scope that followed the Council of Trent. It is worth adding that probably the now stronger Holy Office had an easier time to prosecute wizard-priests than the relatively weak Inquisition of the early sixteenth century, which had often to cope with the solid networks of political and ecclesiastical clientage that protected local clergy.[121]

Tracing the footsteps of wizard-priests is a good way to get a clearer picture of who were, socially and culturally speaking, the lay men who practiced magic in sixteenth-century Modena. Typically, in fact, a priest with his books of demonic magic was the center of groups of people variously participating in the occult arts. The long and complicated trial of Don Campana (1517) reveals the existence of networks of men (and sometimes women) interested in necromancy, who would pool their resources to pursue their more ambitious projects, and often cooperate and exchange books and advice.[122] Usually upper-middle- and middle-class (although aristocrats are not rare), literate, these Modenese wizards belonged to the world of lawyers, merchants, notaries, master craftsmen, and shopkeepers. Their goals ranged from the simple—provoking love—to the more sophisticated—such as becoming invisible or finding hidden treasures.[123] Theirs was a mainly urban setting, and their interests were usually not shaped by pressing everyday needs.

A different typology of techniques, and of magicians, is that documented by cases from the countryside, where the health of people and cattle alike seems to have been of greater concern, and men to have had mainly the role of healers along the lines of folklore remedies. Even in a rural environment, however, a magician's techniques could be shaped by very different cultural traditions, as shown in the trial of Brighento Brighenti (1531), a quack doctor and veterinarian from the country area of Maranello. Brighento, in fact, declared to have learned how to treat epilepsy and apoplexy from a physician he was apprenticed to in his young years, but resorted also to signing, blessed candles, and prayers, that is, the common stock of healing practices of popular origin.[124]

Modenese sorceresses, on the other hand, had a near-monopoly on love magic and fortune-telling, and were equally active as healers. The typology of techniques they practiced shows that normally these were part of the repertoire of traditional popular magic, transmitted orally within the family. Witchcraft was thought of as passing from parents to children, so that in the public's eye a mother's bad reputation as a sorceress amounted to a strong presumption of guilt for her daughter(s), or also son(s). A remarkable example of a "sorcerer's genealogy" is that of Sebastiano della Seca, from the village of Nonantola, accused of having magically sparked the love of the chaste and well-placed Diamante towards himself in 1520. Not only Sebastiano's mother, Maria, and her mother, Cecca, were notorious as witches, but also his uncle, Marco, had been held to be a wicked wizard, and in this latter case the transmission of witch-lore had supposedly taken place via the books that the nephew had inherited.[125]

Magical know-how would frequently circulate between friends and accomplices. At the beginning of the sixteenth century, the Modenese Inquisition investigated several enchantresses who were said to have learned the tricks of the trade in Bologna from a renowned local witch, a certain Cimeria whose execution by the Inquisition there in 1498 had meant for her disciples the road to exile in nearby Modena.[126] Two of them, Costanza Zaccaria and Giulia of Bologna, seemed to have kept in close contact with one another and with Anastasia la Frappona, who confessed to having learned from them several practices. Rarer, but by no means absent, were cases of women who had learned special techniques from written sources or anyway from exchanges with literate magicians: we have already discussed the cases of Bernardina Stadera and, again, of Anastasia, both of whom shared their knowledge with closely associated clergymen. At the end of the sixteenth century, interestingly, the development of the printing industry and the spread of inexpensive broadsheets influenced the ways magical know-how was transmitted. Typical magico-religious prayers such as those of Saint Martha or Saint Daniel began circulating in print form among Modenese prostitutes practicing sorcery along with "books of secrets." These were sort of do-it-yourself handbooks containing descriptions of many remedies based on a mixture of official medical knowledge and magical principles, which were read and exchanged especially among wizard-priests.[127]

A gender connotation is fairly evident in the way magic was practiced in Modena. Women provided both love magic techniques mainly (but not only) to other women, almost always seeking to bind to themselves (ideally through marriage) the "love of their life," and therapeutical remedies to a more mixed clientele, of which children were a major component. Male wizards, on the other hand, were called on generally by other men who did not need magic for marriage purposes, but rather to win the favors of a mistress. In the countryside men were the majority of cattle healers.

This picture changes radically, though, when we consider clergy. Priests and friars, in fact, largely escaped gender distinctions, and performed magical practices of virtually any kind for both male and female customers. Love magic seems to have been a favorite occupation for ecclesiastics (often also for personal use), to the point that in 1589 a Franciscan, Ippolito Scapinelli, could be successfully asked by an acquaintance to teach him love spells with the argument that, "since I [Scapinelli] was a friar, I necessarily had to know some recipes for love magic."[128] Necromancy remained a constant feature of clergy's occupations throughout our period, making ecclesiastics prized consultants for any magical enterprise that required the conjuring of demons. In the last decades of the sixteenth century, the Counter Reformation Church's effort to implement ecclesiastical health remedies as an antidote to magical, superstitious techniques likely lead to an increase of clerically-administered cures, often no less superstitious than those they were supposed to replace. Exorcism, in particular, was refashioned from a method of expelling demons into a simple anticharm, an "ecclesiastical medicine" aimed at counteracting bewitchments caused by human agents. This shift is signaled by the wide diffusion of exorcism handbooks, together with books of secrets, among the Tridentine clergy; and it helps explain the higher frequency with which exorcists were tried for magical practices between the close of the sixteenth century and the first decades of the seventeenth.[129]

APPENDIX

INQUISITION TRIALS AGAINST SORCERESSES
AND MAGICIANS

Notes to the Translations

The original transcripts of the trials are all kept in the State Archives of Modena: Archivio di Stato di Modena, *Inquisizione*, busta 2, Processi 1489-1549, fascicoli I, II, III.

"Busta," or folder, is the individual unit of an archival series—in our case, *Inquisizione*—and is frequently made up of several hundred pages. "Fascicolo," or file, is a subdivision of a "busta;" it usually includes a number of trials carried out by different judges, generally (but not always) over consecutive periods.

Omissions
... Three ellipsis dots signal the omission of a part of a sentence of the original document.
(...) Three dots enclosed in parentheses are used when whole sentences, or several paragraphs, are omitted.

Interpolations and illegible words
( ) Missing or illegible words are indicated by a blank space enclosed in parentheses.
[word] Words enclosed in brackets are an integration of the original text, meant either to add what was left out mistakenly by those who wrote it, or to aid the comprehension of the document.

Italic text is used for comments or headings added by the author, and for a few cases of titles of books mentioned in the original.

The spelling of names has been modernized. Punctuation, almost entirely absent in the original, has been added or modernized.

Bernardina Stadera and the Demon in the Glass Sphere

Deposition of Don Jacopo Pelloni, 23 October 1499

Don Jacopo Pelloni, citizen of Modena living in the cinquantina[1] of San Bartolomeo, son of Marchione Mezardi, summoned by the municipal messenger Pellegrino de Albertini, presented himself before Friar Gregorio of Modena, vicar general of the office of the Inquisition of heretical depravity in the city of Modena and its diocese. (...)

Interrogated whether he knows Bernardina Stadera, wife of Jacopo Stadera, living in the parish of San Bartolomeo of Modena, he answered he does.

Interrogated how does he know her, he answered that he has eaten and spoken with her many times in his house and elsewhere.

Interrogated whether she does or knows anything which is contrary to the [Christian] faith, he answered she does. In fact, during last summer, on a day and month he does not remember, in his house and in the presence of Don Geminiano Calandrino, from the cinquantina of San Pietro of Modena, the said Bernardina made paper figurines of two children and put them on a table and took a bowl filled with spring water and a sword, and she touched the water with the sword's point saying some words in such a low voice, that neither the said witness nor the said Don Geminiano could understand. Bernardina kneeled while pronouncing silently those words, and she intended to make him see whether his mistress loved him or not. Those paper figurines were tied with a hair, and were lying down before she said those words, but as soon as she spoke they stood up without anyone touching them, rather, "they rose up by themselves."[2] (...)

Further, he said that he has heard from many people, and particularly from his sister, that Don Antonio de Montagnana, nephew of the late bishop,[3] is believed to have given to the said Bernardina some holy oil and chrism to perform malevolent magic. (...)

Further, he said he has heard, but does not remember from whom, that the said Bernardina had those figurines baptized, even though he does not know who baptized them. However, it is believed that Don Alberto Zavarisio, nephew of Don Giuliano Zavarisio, parish priest of San Giorgio in Modena, baptized those figurines ( ) [since he was on] most friendly terms with the same Bernardina.

Further, he said that the said Bernardina told him she keeps a devil at her service in a glass sphere, and that his brother Gaspare has seen and held it in his hands. According to Gaspare, that glass sphere felt light as he first took it with his hand, then shortly afterwards it became so heavy, that he could not hold it anymore, and threw it in Bernardina's lap. The evil spirit in that glass sphere belonged to the aforementioned late bishop, according to what Gaspare and Bernardina said.

Further, he said that about three months ago, in the church and convent of the Servite friars, he heard from Friar Sebastiano, Friar Marco and Friar Evangelista, that the said Bernardina sent through her daughter Barbara three hosts, on which some words were written, but he does not know what words. He does know, however, that these words were written in red, and that it is believed that they had been written with blood. (...)

Deposition of Bernardina Stadera, 2 December 1499

... Bernardina wife of Jacopo Stadera from the village of San Bartolomeo of Modena ... interrogated whether she knows anything which is against the Catholic faith about Friar Sebastiano of Modena, of the Order of the Servites, answered he has a book of paper, handwritten, with a white leather binding, of average size, which he lent to her. She kept that book for six months, meaning to copy what was in it, even though she never did because she had been very busy. She anyway read that book many and many times, and found how to make [wax] images and in what way they have to be baptized by a priest to make people love each other, as well as how to curse the mass by saying, "You're lying in your throat"[4] when the priest says, "May the Lord be with you," as she thinks. There was also a conjuration which included the names of many saints, mixed with several names of demons.

Further, she deposed that in that year 1499, in July, in the presence of the same witness, of Don Antonio Montagnana, and of the brother of Don Guglielmo Campana,[5] the said Don Guglielmo,[6] parish priest of San Michele, showed her a book, the size of a sheet of a missal, bound in wood and red or white leather, and read from it many conjurations, and how it was necessary to observe good and bad days. And he told them that by using an incantation included in that book, he could conjure a devil to come into a crystal phial and to speak.

Further, she deposed that Don Giovanni Gualengo showed her a leather-bound book written on paper, in which the said witness believes there were some superstitious things to make oneself loved. (...)

Deposition of Giovanna Mascarelli, 8 December 1499

The respectable woman Giovanna, wife of Gaspare Mascarelli ... presented herself before Friar Gregorio of Modena, of the Order of the Friars Preachers,[7] general vicar of the office of the Inquisition. (...)

[She said that] the said Bernardina showed her several times one crystal vase, about one finger long, in which Bernardina claimed was enclosed the spirit of Ettore Galeazzi. Bernardina used to carry that vase sometimes to her hip and sometimes in her bosom, and she had obtained that spirit in the following way, according to what she herself told the present witness. As a certain man by the name of Ettore Galeazzi laid mortally ill at San Lazzaro near Modena,[8] the aforementioned Bernardina used to go to him on a daily basis for a month, and urged him to give her that crystal vase, in which Galeazzi kept a devil. She was so insistent, that Galeazzi in the end gave her the vase with the spirit.

Interrogated whether the said Bernardina told her that she spoke with the devil every night, she answered she did, meaning she spoke every night with the said spirit of Ettore Galeazzi. (...)

Interrogated whether the said Bernardina told her that she wanted to know from that spirit past and completely unknown events, she answered she did. (...)

Further, since Gaspar, husband of the present witness, was living in Genoa at that time, that is, in 1497, the said Bernardina told her, "Tomorrow I'll be able to tell you what your husband is doing and how he is." And then Bernardina would ask that spirit, and the spirit would answer her in a certain way. Then the following day Bernardina went to the present witness and told her, "At present there is something wrong with your husband Gaspar: he has another woman." Bernardina would also foretell future events as she would get them from the spirit ...

The said Bernardina told her that the Bishop Montagnana had a small bottle, in which he kept a spirit, and when Bernardina would bring the said spirit of Ettore Galeazzi close to that small bottle, then the spirit kept by the said Bishop Montagnana would get all cloudy, while the spirit of Galeazzi would not. [Giovanna] also said that Bernadina's younger son Bartolomeo told her that he prized that spirit of Galeazzi more than he would a good property.

The said Bernardina told the present witness that she wanted to go at night on the rooftop of the witness' house, if she agreed, to conjure up demons, but Giovanna refused. (...)

Interrogated about Bernardina's reputation, she answered she is notorious for being shameless, a procuress and a sorceress.

Deposition of Mrs. Francesca Tosabecchi, 4 January 1499

Mrs. Francesca, wife of the notary Ser Ottaviano Tosabecchi, having been summoned presented herself before friar Gregorio of Modena. (...)

Interrogated whether she knows that the said Bernardina has done or said anything against the Catholic faith, she answered that once, when Bernardina was in the house of the said Ser Ottaviano and of the present witness, in the presence of the noblewoman Lucrezia,[9] wife of the Marquis of Carrara and daughter of the magnificent Lord Sigismondo, brother of the magnificent and illustrious Lord Ercole d'Este Duke of Ferrara, and of Lady Orsolina Sadoleto, wife of Lord Niccolò Sadoleto,[10] Bernardina, speaking with them, said she kept a spirit "to her orders."[11] (...)

The inquisitor apparently did not follow through the accusations against Bernardina, as the proceedings end with no trace of a verdict.

Notes

1. In medieval and early modern Modena the "cinquantina" was a subdivision of a neighborhood.

2. The words between quotation marks are in the Modenese vernacular in the original.

3. Jacopo Sandri of Montagnana, suffragan bishop of Modena at the end of the fifteenth century.

4. The words between quotation marks are in the Modenese vernacular in the original.

5. Andrea Campana, brother of Don Guglielmo, was involved in magical practices and was investigated by Modena's inquisitor in 1517.

6. The best-known sorcerer in early sixteenth-century Modena (see above, p. 51).

7. I.e. of the Dominican order (Dominicans were known as Friars Preachers).

8. A reference to the old hospital for contagious diseases, the lazaretto, (Italian "lazzaretto"), which stood next to the Church of San Lazzaro, in the eastern suburbs of Modena.

9. Lucrezia d'Este, niece of Duke Ercole I of Ferrara and wife of Alberigo Malaspina, Marquis of Massa and Carrara.

10. Niccolò Sadoleto was a member of one of the most prominent families of the Modenese patriciate.

11. The words between quotation marks are in the Modenese vernacular in the original.

A Fearsome Wizard-Priest: Don Guglielmo Campana

Complete Trial against Don Guglielmo Campana, Modenese priest, rector of the parish church of San Michele, most wicked man and conjurer of a demon.[1]

Deposition of Lucrezia Pasini, nicknamed "Gotola," 13 January 1517

Lucrezia, daughter of the late Antonio Benci, wife of Antonio "Gotola," appeared before the father vicar of the Inquisition, and denounced to the same inquisitor that since about eighteen years ago she has been having, and still has, a demonic spirit in her right thigh. During this time she has frequently experienced nocturnal visions, and although she tried many different remedies, she could never be healed nor released.

She was finally persuaded to go and talk to Don Guglielmo Campana, asking him to deliver her. Don Guglielmo thus came to her house, many times read words over her—though she did not understand them—and told her to come to his parish Church of San Michele. She therefore went there numerous times, and once Don Guglielmo took her before the main altar, had her sit, then drew a circle on the ground, which she then entered while the said Don Guglielmo softly hit her garments with a bundle of olive branches, reciting some words she cannot remember. At this point the demonic spirit vexing her said to Don Guglielmo, "Do what you have to do."[2] Then Don Guglielmo took some sulphur, put it on the fire and fumigated the face of the said woman. (...)

Further, she said that the same Don Guglielmo asked her several times to commit sin with him. ... Adding that once, as she was going to the cathedral and was passing by the graveyard of San Michele, the said priest followed her, telling her, "Don't you want to give me respite from my sufferings, I will make you come, in spite of you," meaning to his house, "and I will make you [become] possessed once again, as happened to that person in the Church of San Girolamo, and the whole town will run after you."[3]

Further, [Lucrezia said] that on the day of Saint Blaise[4] the aforesaid witness, asked by the said Don Guglielmo, went to the Church of San Michele and was given a blessed candle by the same priest, who told her: "What do you think, that it was I who put a spell on you? Of course I was the one who did it ... because such things cannot be done but by clergy. And I did this because of the great love I have for you." (...)

Further, [Lucrezia] testifies that a certain Diamante de Funo told her that Don Giovanni Albrisi, priest of Modena, once said to the same Diamante that he could not deliver the aforementioned Lucrezia, because the said Don Guglielmo had enchanted and bound on the same woman the devil Astaroth.[5]

Further, she said that Pietro Merlo, weeder, once told her that Don Guglielmo is a scoundrel, and that he knows well his evil deeds and incantations. He said that once, at night time, he was led by the same Don Guglielmo to the grave of a certain Samano, and that the said priest read from some book of his, and while he read he said to the same Pietro, "Dig here." This he did, and they eventually found the corpse of the said Samano, and Don Guglielmo took three nerves from the neck of the corpse. [Pietro also said that] the same Don Guglielmo kept a human skull, and that he used to scratch from that skull to get some powder, which he would give in broth to bewitched people. (...)

First interrogation of Don Campana, 17 January 1517

The venerable Don Guglielmo Campana, Modenese priest, appeared spontaneously before the Reverend Father Friar Antonio da Brescia, deputy inquisitor in the city of Modena ... within the deadline set in the edict issued by the said inquisitor on Christmas day, 1516[6] ... and swore in due form over the Gospels to say simply and truly whether he had erred against the faith or against anything pertaining to the office of the Inquisition ...

Don Guglielmo said that he has gained in town the infamous reputation of having a familiar demon, while in reality he never had a demon. What actually happened was that when sometimes women would come to him, asking to know whether their husband or lover still loved them, he, wanting to satisfy their curiosity and to draw some of them to his unchaste desire, took them in a secluded part of his house, and had a man hidden in a secret place there, who would give responses—as demons do—to the same Don Guglielmo and to the women. To this end he was helped by Don Pellegrino Valla, a Modenese priest now living in Parma.

Interrogated by the said deputy inquisitor whether [Don Guglielmo] had those women kneel before, or worship, or make offerings to, such person giving responses, whom the women believed to be the devil, he answered no, but he only had those women say some church prayer before the said conversation [with the demon], so that they would not be afraid. (...)

[Don Guglielmo] said he did all this many times, more than twenty times, and that is why he believes to have been disgraced, because those women have said to other people that he had made them speak with a devil, whom they thought he kept in his service.

Interrogated if he ever cast any spell, he answered that once he was asked by a certain woman, who lamented her husband's estrangement, to make her some magical slips containing the prayer of Epiphany written with her blood, so that her husband would love her again. Then Don Guglielmo wrote that slip with the aforesaid prayer in blood extracted from a finger of that woman, and gave it to her. This he did because that woman bothered him.

Further, he said that once, while in Bologna, he was asked by a certain woman, sister of the bishop of Ventimiglia, to charm one aching tooth of hers. He drew the sign of the cross on her side with a knife, then he touched the woman's tooth with the knife saying, "May the tooth's pain be as sweet as the milk that the Virgin Mary gave to Our Lord Jesus Christ." And as soon as he did that, she said the toothache ceased. (...)

Interrogated whether he ever had any book containing charms and conjurings, he answered that he once had a book from a certain man from Cremona, whose name he does not know. In that book charms, incantations and many 'experimenta'[7] were contained. He kept the book for three months, then about four years ago gave it to a cleric, and never got it back.

Interrogated whether he ever gave to anyone any magical slips to provoke love or some other effect, he answered that women would often come to him, bothering him in order to have some slips for the said purposes, and he would then write on these slips the first words that would come to his mind. He never wrote diabolical characters, nor names of demons or other unknown names; he remembers specifically having written on one such slip the following words, "As there was peace between Christ and his disciples, so may there be peace between such-and-such man and such-and-such woman," meaning the persons nominated. On other slips he wrote the names of good angels. (...)

Adding that sometimes he would advise women who could not have sexual intercourse with their men to take quicksilver, put it in some wax, tie it to their arms, and then have sex with their men.

Further, he said he once did this experiment to know whether a person was possessed by the devil: he took a branch from an olive tree, and drew three circles around those who were said to be vexed by a demon. While drawing those circles, he recited some prayers taken from his books.

[Don Guglielmo] also consigned all his books, numbering six, to the same father inquisitor ... in order that he examine and correct them, if they contain any error.

Adding [Don Guglielmo] that to know whether a spell had been cast on a person, he used to perform this experiment: first, he would measure the person's waist, then he would recite some prayer, then would measure the waist again. When he would find that waist to be diminished, he would know that the said person had been charmed, and would often read prayers to these persons.

Adding further that to the said charmed persons he would give also some medicine, but he would always consult beforehand with a physician or an apothecary, and those medicines would never contain anything but the things appropriate for that disease, which other doctors use in similar cases, and he would never say any words nor do any superstitious deeds with these medicines. (...)

Interrogated whether he gave any powder to children suffering from the falling sickness,[8] he answered yes, that is, he gave to those children powder of coral and peony in milk to drink, and this without any superstition. And [Don Guglielmo] also signed epileptic children and adults with a blessed candle, reciting prayers from the aforesaid books. (...)

Interrogated whether he ever went to pick the seeds of the fern on Saint John the Baptist's night,[9] and with whom, he answered he had gone more than ten times, with Francesco Resina and his servant. And [Don Guglielmo] said that, to pick those seeds, he used four sheets of paper, on which he had written the following quotes from the Gospels, "In the beginning was the Word," "Roll of the genealogy," "Jesus was led out into the desert," "In the days of King Herod."[10] And he put the sheets with these quotes on the ground under plants of fern, and in this way sometimes he would find grains of fern, sometimes he would not...

Interrogated what did he do with the aforesaid seeds, he answered he gave them to the children ill with the falling sickness, in order that they wear them around their neck. (...)

Interrogated whether he ever doubted, or said anything against the faith, or did anything against the faith or anything against the office of the Inquisition, answered no, rather [he says that] about all that in which he seems to have erred he has said the mere, simple and pure truth, and that he is a true Christian and wants to be against the demons, and to have no commerce nor familiarity with them.

Interrogated whether he confesses once a year, he answered that he confesses two or three times a week, namely when he wants to celebrate mass. (...)

Second interrogation of Campana, 22 January 1517

(...)

[Campana] said he had thought over his doings, and now remembered that about three years ago he was called and required by Sir Bernardino Marescotti to go to Bologna, to see whether a woman, who lived in that city, was vexed and possessed by a diabolical spirit or not[11]. He therefore went to Bologna together with Giovanni Tassoni,[12] with the same Sir Bernardino and with others he does not remember. He saw the woman and asked her with conjurations to tell the truth, whether in a place called Confortino, an estate of the same Marescotti family in the Bolognese countryside, a treasure was hidden or not. She answered that a hidden treasure was in fact there, meaning in the aforesaid place. Therefore the said Don Guglielmo and the above mentioned went to the said place, and the said Bernardino searched for the treasure, conducting excavations in a certain location there, but nothing was found then.

Questioned whether he himself had done any incantation, Don Guglielmo answered no, and that likewise he had not read any prayers to find the aforesaid treasure, nor had conjured any demons, rather he celebrated mass daily in a certain chapel there, and prayed God alone that He let them find the treasure if this was for the better, and that He would not let storms come. (...)

Summary of the charges against Don Guglielmo, drafted by the vicar of the Inquisition of Modena, Friar Antonio da Brescia, 4 March 1517

This is the investigation that will be carried out by Friar Antonio da Brescia, vicar of the Inquisition in the city and diocese of Modena, sitting as judge in the room of his residence, in force of his duty, authority and power, ... against Don Guglielmo Campana, Modenese priest, rector of the Church of San Michele in Modena, citizen and inhabitant of Modena, ... who ... on account of the things he did and said, has departed from the path of the true Catholic faith, having before his eyes not God, but rather the Enemy of human nature, and especially on account of evil invocations and consultations of demons, prayers offered to the same demons, offerings promised and given, wax images made to cast *maleficium*, slips of paper written with formulas, done so that through these maleficent incantations [the devil] might change the will and thought of people, either by placing [these spells] under the bed in which they sleep, or under the threshold of their houses, and on account of many other superstitious and condemned practices, with which he has deflected from the common life habits of the faithful. (...)

Fourth interrogation of Don Campana, 12 March 1517

(...)

Asked whether he ever kept any familiar spirit, he answered he did keep one constrained in a crystal ball, which he got from Don Antonio Montagna from Modena,[13] and he kept it for about five years. He does not have it any longer, though, since he gave it to Don Geminiano Magnanini four years ago.

Asked whether he ever got responses from the said spirit, he answered he did, several times.

Asked how he managed to get responses from it, either by worshipping it as a deity, or by resorting to some superstition, or by making a pact with that spirit, he answered he did not do any of that, but he would simply put on the surplice and the stole and would order the spirit [to give a response] with the exorcisms that are commonly used against demons. (...)

Further, he said he gave to his clients some powder made of skull bone, that is, from the head of a dead person, mixed with some other components, to treat epilepsy, and he did so with no other superstitious act. (...)

Further, he said that, when he went to Confortino with Sir Bernardino Marescotti and Giovanni Tassoni to look for the hidden treasure, he would bless the place where the treasure was searched for with holy water, and would conjure demons—without any superstition—so they would not stop the hunt for the treasure. He would then take two rods, on which he wrote the words, "Christ wins, Christ reigns," and would hold them one across the other saying the following words, "Behold, thou desirest truth in the inward being,"[14] so that the power of the rods would indicate where the treasure was located. He said that the rods did point to the treasure, but he did not find it. (...)

Further, answering to a question he said he once had a book, called *Clavicula Salomonis*, and another book, called *Almandel*, and some other booklets and writings with many love magic instructions, and he said he burned them all ... but those six he handed in to the father vicar of the Inquisition in Modena.

Asked whether he knows anything of interest to the office of the Inquisition concerning Don Zanone de Albrisiis de fra Albertino, Modenese priest,[15] he answered he thought him to be a bad man about these things since the said Don Zanone uses books which contain excerpts from the *Clavicula Salomonis* and that once, about twenty years ago, when Sir Pietro Paolo Valentini and Sir Filippo Bellincini wanted to consecrate a certain book, Don Zanone celebrated several masses on that book in the palace of Sir Ludovico Bellincini.[16] (...)

List of crimes committed by Don Campana, read out loud by an Inquisition official from the pulpit of the Church of San Domenico at the moment of Campana's abjuration and condemnation, 5 April 1517[17]

These are the things that Don Guglielmo Campana has confessed to and ratified without torture[18] in his trial conducted by the father vicar of the Inquisition.

First of all, for about five years he kept a diabolical spirit constrained in a crystal ball, from which spirit Don Guglielmo asked and received responses about both present things and future, contingent events.

Further, he has conjured the devil through incantations, in order that he give him responses on several things.

Further, he personally made, and taught and helped others to make, many wax dolls, writing on the said images names of devils and sticking a pin where their heart would have been. Sometimes he heated these dolls on the fire, sometimes he threw them in the water. He did all this to provoke illicit love. Then he conjured devils in order that they change the mind of those persons, hoping to get such things done thanks to the devils.

Further, he wrote on paper, on tree leaves and many other such things, names of devils, several magical characters and many unknown names and many charms in order to provoke love, hoping that the demons would have changed the feelings of people and expecting those devils to carry out such work.

Further, he taught a recipe to provoke hate between different persons, taking an egg and using many superstitions and feeding it to a dog and a cat.

Further, he cheated about twenty women, pretending to make them speak with the devil. It was actually a man, who spoke and gave responses as if he were the devil. In this way he taught and persuaded these women to offer a sacrifice to the devil by means of sexual intercourse. Thus he has had sex with about twelve women, who believed to truly make an offering to the devil through this act. Then the said priest had those women bring the cloth which they had used to clean their private parts to the church's altar, as a sacrifice to the devil.

Further, he taught several people to do various magical experiments to provoke love, invoking and conjuring several demons.

Further, he dressed a woman in a priestly robe before the altar of the Church of San Michele, and pricked her ring finger, and used the blood to write demonic incantations on a slip of paper to stir up love.

Further, he kept for a long time several heretical books, censured by the Holy Mother Church.

Further, he used words from Holy Scriptures, and other holy words, to make magical slips to stir up love.

Further, he used the four Gospels to pick the seeds of the fern, on the night of Saint John the Baptist; then he used the seeds for many things, and especially to gain favor.

Further, he made, and taught to make, some pastry with milk from a mother and a daughter, with many superstitions, to provoke love. (...)

Don Campana was found guilty of heresy for having conjured the devil and having made offerings to him in order to foretell future events and to obtain the fulfillment of his plans. He was condemned to life imprisonment, but assigned the city of Modena as a prison. He was also condemned to fast on bread and water, prohibited to celebrate mass, and obligated to appear before the inquisitor once a month, for a year. The inquisitor forbade him to confess, cure, and exorcize for the rest of his life, and condemned him to pay the trial's expenses. However, Don Campana appealed to the Apostolic Penitentiary and the following year was absolved of all his errors and declared fit to perform his priestly duties as before.

Notes

1. *This is the unusually long heading written by an official of the Inquisition on the cover of the trial's folder.*

2. *This and all following passages between double quotation marks are in the Modenese vernacular in the original, unless otherwise specifically indicated.*

3. *This is probably a reference to an otherwise unknown episode of demonic possession in Modena.*

4. *Saint Blaise was frequently invoked against throat diseases, and—as clarified in a later passage of this deposition—Lucrezia sometimes felt the demon vexing her to be in her throat.*

5. *Don Giovanni Albrisi was appointed exorcist of the cathedral of Modena after Don Guglielmo's removal from that office during his Inquisition trial in 1517. The name of the devil Astaroth is found in several books of necromancy that provide instructions on how to conjure him.*

6. *A reference to the "time of grace." See above, pp. 23-24.*

7. *This Latin term was typically used in medieval books of magic with the meaning of "magical recipe;" see Eamon 1994, 56-59.*

8. *Epilepsy.*

9. *24 June, Midsummer night.*

10. *The quotes (all in Latin in the original) are Jn 1:1, Mt 1:1, Mt 4:1, Lk 1:5, respectively.*

11. *Bernardino Marescotti, from Bologna, belonged to a prominent family of the local aristocracy.*

12. *Giovanni Tassoni, a habitual client and accomplice of Campana's magical practices, was a Modenese patrician from a wealthy and well-connected family.*

13. *Don Antonio Montagnana, nephew of the suffragan bishop of Modena (Jacopo Sandri da Montagnana), lover and accomplice of the witch Bernardina Stadera (see above, p. 48).*

14. *Ps. 51:6 (Ps. 50:8 in the Vulgate).*

15. *See above, note 5.*

16. Both the Valentini and the Bellincini families belonged to the upper levels of Modenese society. Ludovico Bellincini was a well-known lawyer who also served as a consultant to the inquisitor of Modena.

17. The text of the list was in the Italian vernacular, clearly in order to be understood by, and to serve as a warning to, the audience that had come to attend the conclusion of Campana's trial.

18. "Without torture:" this expression did not mean that the defendant had not been tortured (Campana in fact had been), but rather that the confession obtained through torture had been ratified by the defendant the next day in a room different from the torture chamber (therefore presumably without fear of being tortured again).

Saints and Devils: Costanza "Barbetta" and Her Spells

Deposition of Laura Betocchia, 28 December 1518

(...)

Questioned how does she know that [Costanza] has a bad reputation and [is known to be] a sorceress, she answered that with her own eyes saw her buying wood in the name of the great devil, and putting a horseshoe from a horse's left fore hoof in the name of the great devil on that wood set on fire, and hitting an odd number of times the afore-mentioned horseshoe with a hammer in the name of the great devil, and while she hit the hammer she would say,[1] "I do not hammer and hit you, horseshoe, rather I hit the heart, mind, imagination, feelings and vigor of Barbetta."[2] Then she used to take that horseshoe and to cool it for a little while in a chamber pot with urine, saying these words, "I do not let sizzle you, horseshoe, but rather the mind, heart, vigor and feel-ings of Barbetta, until he comes to this house to do as I please." Then she used to hit the horseshoe again on the fire, and would repeat all these things until that man was forced to come to her house. And when he was ill, he was obliged to send someone else in his place.

Questioned how does she know that the man was forced to go or to send someone else in his place, she answered that she had seen all this happening more than ten times with her own eyes, and the same Barbetta forced to come in the aforementioned way. She added that when Barbetta would come, he looked half dead and extremely tor-mented and afflicted.

Questioned whether the aforesaid Costanza seemed to put great trust in those diabolical works of hers and in the same devil she conjured, she answered to have heard from the same Costanza that she believed in these things in a most stunning way. (...)

Questioned whether she knows anything else about the aforesaid Costanza concerning such conjurings of demons, she answered that innumerable times, perhaps as many as one hundred times, she saw the same Costanza putting her five fingers in five links of the chain in the fireplace, and invoking five demons, saying: "Five fingers I put to the wall, o five devils, I conjure you." Costanza called the demons by their individual names, and while conjuring them she used to say many other words, often inserting the names of the most holy Trinity, Father, Son, and Holy Ghost, without which, as the said witness heard from the same Costanza, she could not have done anything. With that conjuration Costanza also ordered those demons to extract five drops of blood from Barbetta's heart, three of which they had to bring to the same Costanza, while they could keep the other two as a reward.

Deposition of Laura Betocchia, 29 December 1518

(...)
Questioned whether she knows anything else about the said Costanza, she replied that the said defendant used to resort to another spell, which she herself says is very powerful. She takes thirty-three blessed candles and keeps them lit for thirty-three mornings, reciting a prayer she calls of Saint Daniel. According to the said witness, such prayer includes numberless conjurations which call on the name of the person for whom all this was done,[3] thus saying, "Filippo for the Passion of Christ, Filippo for the nails, Filippo for the slaps, Filippo for the crown of thorns," and in the same way she called out Filippo in the name of every single mystery and in the same way she also invoked it for the sun and the moon and the stars and the elements and for various foods, bread, wine, salt and the like, calling out the individual names of all these things and many others, like the pope, the cardinals, the bishops and all the orders of priests, and she conjured it also for the masses celebrated in Rome by bishops and archbishops, and for those which were celebrated on Christmas night and at Easter. She would also throw some long and narrow beans, called "cappodoghe," picked on Saint John the Baptist's day and baptized, in which she had put bread and alum and blessed wax. And she [Costanza] says that by shaking these beans in her hands and by biting some of them, she knows whether the man for whom she does these things is as lovesick as she desires.

The said Costanza also told the present witness that through such rituals and beans and candles and prayers she forced the aforementioned Filippo to go from the citadel of Concordia all the way to Bologna to see her.[4]

She [the witness] added also that the said Costanza had fully learned the aforementioned prayer from a certain woman through the mediation of Mrs. Maddalena, wife of Ludovico Cozzi, Modenese citizen and innkeeper, when Maddalena promised to the said Costanza that a certain woman would have taught her this prayer, as in fact she did in the house of the said Maddalena.

Questioned as to the name of that woman, she says she does not know. (...)

... the said witness [Maria] heard from Laura Betocchia that the said Costanza could teach her how to be loved by a certain lover of hers. Therefore upon request from the same Maria, the aforesaid Costanza taught the said witness to steal a pin in the name of Lucifer, prince of the demons, saying these words, "I do not steal a pin or other things, rather I steal the heart, feelings, vigor and will," naming the man to whom this was meant to be done. Then she added, "May this prevent him from loving, having sex with, and even looking at, all other women, until he comes to do as I, such-and-such," naming the person who was casting the spell, "please and desire." Then [Costanza taught her] to stick the pin in the hem of a dress which she normally wore, saying these words: "I do not stick a pin in woolcloth, nor in linen cloth, nor in sackcloth, nor in felt nor in other things, rather it is an arrow that I strike at the heart of such-and-such," naming the person to whom all this was done. And she concluded in this way: "May this deprive him of heart, feelings, vigor and will [and prevent him from] loving, having sex with, and even looking at, all other women, in the name of Lucifer, greatest devil and master of Hell."

[Maria] testified that Costanza would then teach her to measure the hem of the said dress for five times and [she would find it to be] five spans; then she had to hold one end of the said dress and to measure it again, and she would find it now to be a little longer than four spans or circa; and this was a sign that she had achieved her aim through the aforementioned superstitions. [Costanza] taught her that while measuring it the second time, she had to say these words: "I do not span woolcloth, nor linen cloth, nor sackcloth, nor felt or other things, rather I span the heart, mind, vigor, feelings and will, and [thus I prevent him from] loving, looking at and having sex with, all other women, until he come to me such-and-such, to say and do that which I will tell and command him in the name of Lucifer, greatest devil of Hell." Then she would add, "May you such-and-such run more than any horse ever did, in the name of me such-and-such, in the name of Lucifer, greatest devil, master of Hell." (...)

After a consultation with fellow friars and with the notaries of the Inquisition, Giovanni Andrea Guidoni and Giovanni Niccolò Morano, the inquisitor Bartolomeo Spina decided to release Costanza, with the intention of eventually asking the bishop and some lawyers for advice on her case. The Inquisition files, however, contain no further document on Costanza.

Notes

1. This and all following passages between quotation marks are in the Modenese vernacular in the original.
2. Filippo Barbetta, Costanza's lover, whose last name became the woman's nickname.
3. Filippo Barbetta.
4. Concordia sulla Secchia, north of Modena, is about fifty-five miles from Bologna.

Anastasia "la Frappona," the Enchantress

Deposition of Eleonora Mantovani, 24 January 1519

Eleonora ... testified that Anastasia has a bad reputation about the magic arts and diabolical superstitions. (...)

Questioned how does she know it, she replied that she knows it because the said Frappona has lived in her house for a year, and they even slept together, so that the said witness would see almost daily many men and women coming to have superstitious remedies for love from her.[1] And she would do that, thus earning much money from many people. (...)

Questioned whether she ever saw her praying in an unusual way, she replied that once, when she was sleeping with her, she saw her kneeling in the middle of the room completely naked, with her hair loose falling down to her waist.

Questioned whom was she praying to then, she replied that Anastasia uttered some words, but she did not understand also because she was not paying attention.

Questioned whether she had then a blessed candle in her hand, she replied that one blessed candle was lighted before the image of the crucifix.

Questioned whether she knows why she would pray kneeling in that way, she replied that she learned eventually from said Frappona that she had done all that to foretell whether a certain man would have married a certain woman, as that woman desired. She had done thus also so that she could see that man, and to know what clothes he would wear, and the said Frappona said to the witness that she knew all these things as she wanted. (...)

Questioned whether she knows how the said defendant manages to know such things, she replied that the same Frappona told her that she would know these things because she would see at night in a vision that man—for whom all this was done—in a large flowery meadow, where a dining table was prepared.

Questioned whether she knows of any other superstitious thing done by her, she replied that she heard from the lips of the same defendant that the same Frappona used to go naked onto the house's roof to pray as she had prayed kneeling in her room. She adds that her niece, Maria, had once heard from her mother, Giovanna, that the said defendant told Giovanna, "If you want to come with me on the roof, I will show many things to you, too!"

Questioned what are the things that she would see, she replied she does not know. (...)

Deposition of Anastasia da Cutigliano, 11 October 1519

The said defendant Anastasia, summoned before Father Prior Aurelio of Lodi, acting as inquisitor, and before the reverend vicar of the bishop, took oath [of speaking the truth] under pain of being condemned as a relapsed and unrepentant heretic, on the matters contained in the trial lawfully formed against her; and although the time of grace has expired,[2] nevertheless the said father prior promised to use mercy, as long as she speaks the truth most fully.

[Anastasia] said and confessed that an image made of wax was given to her by a certain man; she took it and fumigated it with perfume, then threw a drop of water on it and, having first entered a circle drawn [on the ground] with charcoal, said "I perfume you, spirit of love, so that you may go to the heart of so-and-so!"[3]

Questioned if she used to kneel, she answered she could not remember, adding that she also used to take three pins, and used one of them to strike at the heart of the said image saying these words, "May I so strike at the heart of so-and-so, as I strike here," along with other superstitions, and said she did this about six times.

She also added that having called a certain friar, she received from him a heart made of black wax, with three pins stuck in it, and she said, "I do not strike at this heart, but I strike at the heart of so-and-so in the name of the devil." And this she believes to have done five times.

Further, she said that she once bought a key in the name of the devil, put it in the fire and hit it when still in the fire with a hammer saying these words, "I do not strike at this distaff, but at the heart of so-and-so, in the name of the devil," along with other superstitions. And she said she did it only once. (...)

She took a string, made five knots, each in the name of the devil, saying these words, "I do not knot a string, but the heart of so-and-so in the name of the devil." And she did this three or four times, and then she used to put that string with those five knots out of the window of her home in the name of the devil, saying these words, "May so-and-so not hesitate, as does this string," which was stirred by the wind, meaning always Giulio Fontanella.[4] (...)

Then she said she had an image of the devil painted on paper, then erased that figure with a sword, and threw the powder from the erasure on the said Giulio Fontanella. And all that happened two years ago.

Further, she said that she took a stone that had been thrown to the dogs and that a dog had taken in its mouth, and she had the name of Polissena Tortella[5] and the name of Giulio written on it, then took it in her arms and let it fall to the ground saying these words, "May they so love each other as the dog loves the stone." And this she did once.

Then she took some quicksilver in the name of the devil, and took cats' and dogs' hair and mixed everything with bread, which she put— in the name of the devil—in a place through which Giulio and Polissena had passed, saying these words, "May they so linger together as does quicksilver, and so love each other as do cats and dogs." She added she had learned these and many other things from Francesca, daughter of Domenico Dini.

Further, she said she went in a churchyard over the graves of those dead on that day, and having taken some earth from them said these words, "O you who lie here, you do not know me and I do not know you!" and with that earth went to the house of Polissena Tortella and threw it in the house at night, saying these words, "May thus Giulio know not any love or woman other than myself!" And this was once taught to her by the said Francesca.

Further, she said that she took an egg and cooked it in water from three fountains, then split it with a thread and wrote the name of Giulio on one piece and the name of Polissena on the other, then gave one piece to a dog and the other to a cat, saying these words, "May the two of you love each other as cats and dogs do!" (...)

Further, she took a frog and had her name and that of Giulio written on the frog's back with blood extracted from her middle finger, and threw the ashes made out of that frog over Giulio in the name of the great devil, saying, "In the name of the devil, may he never have rest until he comes to me to do as I please." And that she did once.

Further she said that she had made some focaccia [kind of flat bread] with milk from a mother and a daughter, and she wrote the name of God [on them], and gave them to many people to reconcile estranged lovers. She made this focaccia twice, six pieces each time. (...)

Further, she said she went to Don Guglielmo Campana and got from him a slip of written paper, and that the said Don Guglielmo had her put that slip on the altar at a precise time, and then he started reading from a book and wanted her to reply to every single word he read; these words included God and the name of some demon, or so she thought. And this was four years ago.

Deposition of Anastasia, 15 October 1519

(...)
Questioned whether those things she had said in the previous depositions were true, she answered they were, adding, though, that she had not said other things.

Questioned why in the previous depositions she had not spoken the full truth, she answered that it was on the devil's advice, and because "she feared to be exposed."

Questioned whether the devil had appeared to her, she answered that while in jail, before the last day of September she thought she had seen, between sleeping and waking, some shadow in the shape of the devil which suggested that she hang herself with a sheet on the window bars. The shadow also reproached her for having confessed, and because of that she eventually denied several things when interrogated in the bishop's presence.

She added that about twenty-nine years ago, while she was pregnant and was reprimanded by her mother, and felt very upset because she did not want to get married to her husband, and had an abortion by drinking saffron and fermented (   ), the devil appeared to her, suggesting that she hang herself; she was terrified and did not do it. This apparition was as follows: "While I was downstairs, it seemed to me as if he [the devil] was instigating me to go upstairs and hang myself on the roof beam, and when I got there I saw the devil in the shape of a black shadow, and was frightened and went back."

She added that in the end she thought she could kill that husband of hers, and did everything she could to do it.

Questioned whether she had resolved to speak the truth, she answered yes, crying and asking for mercy. Having heard that, the lord inquisitor told her to speak the full truth about those things she culpably did and thought. (...)

"About three or four years ago, I put on the fire some powder of incense, having first drawn a circle [on the ground] with charcoal and having entered it saying, 'I perfume you, spirit of love, may you go to the heart of Giulio Fontanella,' throwing on a wax doll in the shape of a man some oil of turpentine in which there were three pins, then striking that image with those pins saying, 'May this happen in Giulio's heart!'"

Questioned from whom she had that wax doll, she answered from Mr. Sasso,[6] by whom she had also been taught about that circle and suffumigation, and also about the sticking of pins and all as said, although she said that eventually the same Sasso told the said Anastasia that he had taught her all that just to deceive her. (...)

Further: "I bought an oil lamp in the name of the devil, and I also bought oil and wick in the name of the devil, putting the said oil and wick in the name of the devil into the said oil lamp, lighting it and saying, 'May the heart of Giulio light up just as this oil lamp does in the name of the devil.' (...)

Questioned who taught her such superstition, she answered it was a certain woman nicknamed "la Barbetta."[7]

Further: "About fifteen years ago, on advice from a friar all dressed in black, I drew a heart with charcoal on a wooden door, and then struck it with a knife, saying, 'I do not strike this heart, but the heart of Ludovico in the name of the devil.'" (...)

Further: "About two or three years ago I took savin, bread and salt, I rubbed them together and said, 'I do not rub bread, nor savin nor salt, but I rub the heart of Giulio,' and then threw them in some ashes and struck them with a knife, saying, 'I do not strike bread, nor savin nor salt, but I strike the heart of Giulio.'" (...)

Further: "About two years ago I killed a cat, took out the heart and put it into a small saucepan with three strings in the name of the devil and of Giulio, expecting that, as soon as the saucepan would boil, Giulio would have come to me."

Questioned who taught her such superstition, she answered it was a certain woman called Benedetta, who lived in the house of Caterina Molinari.

Further: "About two or three years ago I took some garbina[8] and some incense and put them in the fire saying, 'I make this perfume to Pantaleario' and to others, whose name I cannot remember, so that Giulio would come to me."

Questioned who did she think Pantaleario was, she answered she thought it was some evil spirit. (...)

Further: "About three or four years ago I had a magnet baptized by a priest using the holy water that the said priest had brought, and I participated as godmother, answering to the priest as one does when a child is baptized, and this in the name of the said Giulio, saying, 'I baptize you, Giulio, in the name of the Father, the Son and the Holy Ghost,' and this so that, by touching the said Giulio with the said magnet, he would love me." (...)

Further: "About twelve years ago I got from a priest a small ampulla, in which there was about two fingers of holy oil, with which I oiled my lips and then kissed the said Annibale so that he would love me."[9] (...)

Further: "About two years ago I got a little holy oil from a priest of San Geminiano,[10] which I had asked to oil my sick eyes. In reality I then oiled my lips with it, and kissed the said Giulio so that he would love me."

Questioned who that priest was, she answered his name was Don Giovanni Francesco Albertini, although she added that the said priest had told her he did not want to give her the oil for any evil end, and that she had to beg him and to insist that she would use it for no other purpose but her sickness.

Further: "About twenty-eight years ago, as I wanted to kill my first husband I gave him some quicksilver in an egg. But, after he drank the rest of the egg, the quicksilver remained in the eggshell. Having seen that I had not achieved my end with that system, to get him out of my way I gave him some powder, which was brought to me by Simone Moceno, who told me to give it to him so that he would have died; which I did."

Questioned whether [her husband] was killed or at least fell ill because of those powders, she answered no, but he died several years later, when a vein in his heart broke because of excessive laughter. (...)

Summary of the charges against Anastasia, drafted by the chief inquisitor of Ferrara and Modena Antonio Beccari, 17 October 1519

This is the investigation that will be carried out by the reverend inquisitor of the city of Modena, Friar Antonio of Ferrara, especially appointed against the heretical depravity by the Holy Apostolic See, sitting as judge on the usual bench, in force of his duty, authority and power, and also by authority of the reverend vicar of the episcopal court, against Anastasia nicknamed la Frappona from Cutigliano, presently living in Modena.

According to previous public reputation, referred not by suspect or ill-willing persons, but rather by honest and trustworthy persons out of zeal for justice and holy faith, not only once but rather many and many times ... the said Anastasia is, and is reputed to be, a most wicked sorceress [performing] spells that savour of apostasy from the Catholic faith and of most nefarious idolatry and abuse of the Church's holy sacraments ... a reputation which was confirmed by thirteen witnesses above any exception and suspicion, [who are] not her mortal enemies[11] ... among which many are relatives of the said defendant, who all testified those things out of zeal for justice and desiring to correct her, and several of them testified to think that the defendant is a scoundrel and that she had committed all sorts of evil deeds, crimes which she herself has admitted several times through her own lawfully made confessions, so that it is manifest she is such a criminal, and specifically:

that she is so vicious, nefarious and cruel, that she did not refrain from taking food especially prepared to provoke an abortion. Furthermore, [she tried] to kill two persons through enchanted food. This latter thing she did three times, as she has confessed under oath twice and lawfully ratified without having been tortured and even without having been shown the torture instruments; although—as she declared—death of those people was not achieved through that enchanted food. (...)

Further, that two qualified witnesses ... testified that, among many other things, it was widespread opinion that the said defendant had killed with her spells her first husband and the wife of a certain noble citizen [Annibale Valentini], and that after the death of her first husband and of the first wife of that nobleman, that same nobleman married the said defendant ... and presumption of all this is increased by the fact that both of them died almost at the same time, and then the marriage of the said nobleman to the defendant followed. Presumption increases also because that noble citizen and the said defendant are of very different social status and because—as witnesses testified—when the said noble citizen was reproached by relatives for bringing shame on himself and on his family through this marriage, he had answered that even if the said defendant had gone to a brothel he would have been forced to follow her. Presumption is increased also by the fact that the said defendant, before both her first husband and the first wife of that noble citizen had died, gave to the same noble citizen something to eat in some pastry, so that she would be loved by him, and to the same end she also kissed the said nobleman abusing of holy oil, eventually committing adultery with him many times. (...)

Further, that she used the sacraments of the Holy Church departing from the common rites and the common habits of the faithful, something that according to the sacred canons entails suspicion of heretical depravity. In fact, the said defendant many and many times has abused the sacraments of baptism and of holy oil, baptizing several times by herself a magnet and the heart of a sparrow, also having a priest baptize the same magnet in the same way and with the same ritual and godparents, with which Christians are baptized ... also breaking and throwing the baptized magnet in a chamberpot, having masses celebrated over the magnet, also using the words of the consecration of the body of Christ our Lord in her superstitious deeds, with great abuse of the sacraments of the Church and to the most serious offence of the majesty of Christ.

Further, she has confessed lawfully and without torture to have performed many idle and most foolish superstitions with several superstitious observances, as for example sometimes with earth taken from a holy place, sometimes with the heart of a sparrow, sometimes with bread and salt and savin, sometimes with the heart of a cat, sometimes with a stone taken from the mouth of a dog, sometimes with strings, that are commonly called "stringhe," sometimes with ashes made out of frogs having had a name inscribed on their backs, sometimes with cooked eggs, sometimes with powder rubbed out from a painted image of the devil, ... sometimes with superstitious slips of paper with the name of a demon, put by a priest on the altar ...

Further, many times she gave superstitious things to eat or to drink to several people, sometimes to entice them to illicit love, sometimes to harm them, for example sometimes giving focaccia, sometimes as they commonly say "gnocchi," sometimes water in which she had washed her feet, sometimes even some of her menses ...

Further, she has committed idolatry many times ... therefore becoming an apostate from the Catholic faith; first of all, having drawn about seven times a circle on the ground with charcoal and having entered in it she fumigated the spirit of love with incense, also throwing—while in that circle—some water over a wax image in the shape of a man, and stinging it with three pins in the name of some nobleman, whom she hoped to draw to herself in that way. Secondly, she also fumigated with incense to an evil spirit called Pantaleario, so that she could draw to herself the said nobleman; and she performed this act of idolatry about four times. Thirdly, she explicitly worshipped a star and prayed to it, and she also taught this—as a heresiarch[12]—to several other people. (...)

Further, that she did very many evil and superstitious acts, explicitly invoking the devil and carrying them out in the name of the devil, and with such superstitious acts she meant ... either to make a man change his mind, or to draw him to herself—something she said happened, since in this way she drew to herself a person that was forced to come. (...)

Further, that since she has committed so many and such serious superstitions in the name of the devil to achieve her ends and has performed those acts of idolatry, there is a strong suspicion that she has made other explicit pacts with the devil, with explicit apostasy from the Catholic faith and taking the devil as her lord, especially since all the other people who are part of such sect do that normally.

Further, she has trampled on the cross and done other nefarious things, which these criminals do.

Abjuration of Anastasia, 28 October 1519

This is the abjuration pronounced by the aforesaid Anastasia la Frappona ... who has confessed as in her trial.[13]

I, Anastasia from Cutigliano, presently living in Modena, personally appearing on trial before you, Father Friar Antonio of Ferrara of the Order of the Friars Preachers, reverend inquisitor of heretical depravity especially appointed by the Holy Apostolic See, touching with my own hands the holy Gospels placed before me, swear that I believe in my heart and profess through my mouth that holy Catholic and apostolic faith which the Holy Roman Church believes, protects and preaches; and I consequently abjure, repeal, abhor and repudiate any heresy, of whatever kind or sect, which may rise against the Holy Mother Church.

Further, I, Anastasia swear that I believe in my heart and profess through my mouth that a Christian faithful cannot worship anyone but the one and only God, creator of heaven and earth, and has to make his offerings to Him alone. I therefore abhor, repeal and abjure that kind and species of heresy and apostasy from the holy Catholic faith through which, following the detestable error of the heathens, one worships and offers suffumigation of incense to the infernal devil, with other condemnable superstitious systems. I also abjure, repeal and abhor that other type of idolatry and apostasy from the Catholic faith through which one worships, and prays to, the stars, as the heathens did, expecting and asking and hoping for a change in human minds and hearts. For a long time I was miserably blinded and entangled in this detestable error on account of my ignorance and malice, and not only was I in that error, but I also tried to teach others such erroneous ways, in offence to the divine majesty, to the scandal of the Holy Church, perdition of my soul and ruin of my neighbor, and because of all that I would deserve the toughest penalty.

Now, however, enlightened by divine benignity I return to the unity of the holy Catholic faith, praying humbly Holy Mother Church that it may mercifully accept me as a penitent, asking for mercy, forgiveness and remission of sins.

Furthermore I, the aforementioned Anastasia, swear to believe in my heart, and profess through my mouth, that holy sacraments are to be treated with all reverence, and used only for the legitimate scope for which they have been instituted by Holy Mother Church, and that the true Christian is not to depart in their use from the common tradition of the faithful. Therefore I abhor, repeal and abjure that condemnable heresy following which ... one uses the holy sacrament of baptism to baptize irrational creatures, and the holy sacrament of chrism[14] for most wicked and illegitimate deeds. (...)

Furthermore I, the aforementioned Anastasia, swear to believe in my heart, and profess through my mouth, that the Christian faithful must not in any way have contact, nor to make an implicit or explicit pact, with the infernal devil, enemy of Christ's faith. [The Christian faithful] must not perform any deeds in name or honor of such diabolical spirit, nor must he expect the completion of his deeds to come from the enemy of Christ's faith. (...)

The judges recognized Anastasia's repentance as sincere, and condemned her to ten years of exile from Modena, to fast on bread and water and recite a prayer to the Virgin Mary on Saturdays for the rest of her life, and to pay her trial's expenses.

Notes

1. It was common in the early modern era to sleep in the same bed with a friend, something which had a social, rather than sexual, meaning. See Cohn and Cohn 1993, 194, 291.

2. See above, pp. 24-25.

3. This and all following passages between double quotation marks are in the Modenese vernacular in the original.

4. Giulio Fontanella was the man Anastasia was in love with.

5. Polissena Tortella was Anastasia's rival in the love affair with Giulio.

6. The Modenese humanist and poet Panfilo Sassi, or Sasso.

7. Costanza Zaccaria, nicknamed Barbetta, from Ferrara, herself tried for sorcery by the Inquisition in 1518 (see above, pp. 95-98).

8. Probably a kind of herb.

9. Annibale Valentini, belonging to a promiment Modenese family, was Anastasia's lover, and eventually husband.

10. Meaning the church of San Geminiano, the cathedral of Modena.

11. See above, p. 25.

12. A heresiarch is defined as the leader of a heretical sect, or someone who has lead others to heresy.

13. Anastasia's abjuration is in the Italian vernacular in the original.

14. I.e. holy oil.

Sebastiano della Seca and the Power of Love Magic

Trial against Sebastiano della Seca, from Nonantola, who is reputed to be a sorcerer like his mother, his grandmother and his uncle.[1]

Deposition of Violante Cattani, 17 April 1520

In the name of the Lord, amen. In the year 1520 after the birth of Our Lord, on the day 17 of April, Violante Cattani from Nonantola,[2] wife of the late Giovanni Ludovico Cattani, presented herself before the Reverend Father Friar Bartolomeo of Pisa,[3] vicar of the Inquisition ... and having taken an oath to tell the truth, gave testimony against Sebastiano della Seca, from Nonantola, [on the fact] that many persons have a very strong suspicion that he is a sorcerer, and that he, among other things, cast a spell on a certain girl, called Diamante, daughter of the late Filippo de Cenno, who lives in Nonantola.

The grounds for such suspicion are, first of all, that the mother of the said Sebastiano, whose name is Maria della Seca, is notorious in Nonantola on account of her spells and for being a witch. Maria's mother, too, called "la Cecca", was held by public opinion to be a sorceress and a witch, and so was Maria's brother, the son of the said Cecca, called "Priest Marco" who died a few years ago from poison and was a most wicked sorcerer, and with his spells caused many girls and other women to go to ruin, as is widely known in Nonantola.

Secondly, that the said Sebastiano was in love with the aforementioned Diamante, and courted her insistently. However, she had no intention of agreeing to marry him, because she did not like him nor was he of her same status. In sum, he did not get a single encouraging word from her, and yet he persevered until Lent of this year. During Lent, however, this girl, who had always been extremely shy and very modest in her words and deeds, began to be carried away by love for Sebastiano, to the point that she could not speak of anything else but him, saying that she absolutely wanted to marry him and nobody else, not even the son of the emperor. As some would reproach her, telling her that he was not of her same status, nor handsome nor good, rather of lowly origins and a most miserable fellow, she insisted that he is most noble, handsome and an excellent person, and retorted to those reproaching her that, in fact, they are vile, wicked scoundrels, protesting with most shameless and insulting words against even her sisters and mother. It even happened once that, on account of all this, she ran after her mother to hit her with a burning ember.

Further, that as she [Diamante] was once called by the said Sebastiano outside of her home, she immediately began to run after him, and could hardly be kept from going out by two women and with the greatest effort, to the point that one of the two felt half dead after such effort.

Further, [Violante] says that the said girl is now very seriously ill on account of the love troubles and the spells she has been suffering from, so that she cannot get out of bed and her very life is at stake. Nevertheless, she continues to be madly in love with him.

Further, the said woman says that another reason why she suspects Sebastiano to be a sorcerer is that, as he was captured by the most illustrious governor,[4] the same governor was asked by some important person not to try the aforementioned Sebastiano on charges of spell casting and magical operations if by chance he had been unjustly defamed in his [the governor's] eyes because of his mother, who is reputed to be a witch.

Interrogated for how long the girl continued to reject the said young man and remained constant in her good will, his harassment notwithstanding, she answered [the girl kept rejecting him] firmly for a year, until Lent time of the present year.

Interrogated whether any other signs show that the said girl had been bewitched by him, she answered that she confirms anything he says, even when it throws dishonor and and shame on her. One example among others: as Violante once was told by someone that the young man had claimed to have gotten Diamante pregnant, the said Diamante immediately confirmed this, even though it is thought to be false. She has also vomited many things which indicate that a terrible spell was put on her. (...)

Deposition of Ludovico Giovanni Gerardi, 18 April 1520

Ludovico Giovanni Gerardi, from Nonantola, presented himself before the father vicar of the Inquisition, Friar Bartolomeo of Pisa, called as a witness.

Having taken oath, he was interrogated whether he knows Sebastiano della Cecca, from Nonantola, to be a sorcerer and to have bewitched Diamante de Cenno from Nonantola. He answered that he believes him to be a sorcerer and a witch, and to have bewitched the said Diamante.

He thinks so also because even Sebastiano's mother, whose name is Maria, is presently held by public opinion to have the same abominable habit [of bewitching], as had his grandmother, called la Cecca, and his uncle, called Don Marco, a great sorcerer whose books are now in Sebastiano's keeping.

[He thinks so] also because Sebastiano had fallen in love with the said Diamante, a girl of most honest soul who rejected him until Lent time. At this point, though, she fell in love and got sick on account of this, and she began to insult and to physically threaten all those people who were against her love affair and reproached her, including her mother and sisters. Once she even said to her mother that she wanted to cut her to pieces, and that she did not want to stay with her family. And since the time she has gotten mad with this, she refuses to recite any prayer, neither the Our Father nor the Hail Mary. (...)

The inquisitor apparently did not follow through the accusations against Sebastiano, as the proceedings end with no trace of a verdict.

Notes

1. This is the heading written by an official of the Inquisition on the first sheet of the trial.

2. Nonantola is a village about five miles north of Modena, the seat of an important Benedictine monastery.

3. Bartolomeo Spina, a prominent theologian and author of an important book on witchcraft (see above, pp. 20, 42-43), was vicar of the Inquisition in Modena 1518-20.

4. The famous Florentine political thinker and historian Francesco Guicciardini (1483-1540), then papal governor of Modena.

A Country Healer: Brighento Brighenti of Maranello

Collective deposition of three witnesses, 27 January 1531

The witnesses unanimously declare to Friar Angelo Valentini, vicar of the Inquisition in Modena, that Brighento de Brighenti from Maranello, is and is said and reputed to belong, by public opinion shared by all honest men of Maranello and of the neighboring communities, to the sect of the witches, and is held to be a sorcerer, and he heals children and all sorts of men and women, and he bewitches all the men, women and animals he wishes. (...)

Interrogated by the inquisitor whether they know anything in particular which may confirm such a reputation, they all answer that the aforesaid Brighento about a month ago was seen by Jacopo de Girardi, who afterwards publicly confirmed that he had seen him, in the hours before dawn, holding an oil lamp and crossing a field coming towards the porch of Jacopo's house, and that his nephew, who is a babe in arms, began to cry and to moan as soon as Brighento got close to the door. And that the said Jacopo, who was digging in his mother's orchard and could not be seen by anyone, and was watching what Brighento wanted to do, saw him acting out of the ordinary, that is, as the child started to cry, Brighento went away. As Brighento got close to the road and to the same Jacopo, the said Jacopo shouted, "Who's there?"[1] and the said [Brighento] said, "Booo!" and departed quickly with the lamp, and he saw him going directly to his house, that is, Brighento's, and thus understood that he was in fact Brighento. (...)

A few days later Jacopo got sick in one of his eyes, and while there are no apparent signs of illness, the eye aches ... and because of the aforementioned things Jacopo called Brighento to heal him. Brighento presently cures him, and Jacopo feels almost delivered. (...)

Interrogated about the system he uses to heal, they all answered that he makes [sick people] watch with a light during the night and, as they say, "he signs them."

Interrogated whether they know anything else about his healing method, they answered that he asks money for candles from sick people, and he signs them, and makes people watch over them. (...)

[They added] that the aforementioned Brighento seems not to care about being known as a sorcerer, and he himself admits going to the sabbat, although he appears to have said that jokingly. (...)

Brighento de Brighenti, from the village of Maranello, denounced, summoned, sworn in due form to tell the truth about himself and others. (...)

Interrogated where he had stayed during his life, he answered that about twenty-nine years ago he had lived in Rome for about seven years in the service of a certain physician, whose name was Master Marianus Teutonic. And he was then about thirty-five years old, and that the said Master Marianus treated swellings, pains or aches, and apoplexy and epilepsy.

Interrogated whether he had learned anything from him, he answered that he learned to heal apoplexy, which he treats with one pigeon which he quarters alive and puts on the head of the sick person, and finally he puts a heated brick on the head, and he cures in this way. He also learned to treat the pangs of death, also the cows' backache and swellings and other illnesses of this type.

Interrogated in what way he treats these illnesses, he answered that he cures them with regular medicines, bought from apothecaries, and in no other way.

Interrogated whether, in the places he had lived in, he ever heard talking about, or knew, or personally met, anyone who went to the sabbat, that is, a sorcerer, he answered that he heard talking about [sorcerers] but knew nothing about it, except that he heard say that the friars of St. Dominic burned a certain witch, and used to burn witches.

Interrogated whether he believed anything on matters of witches and sorcerers, as, for instance, that they can harm or do good to animals or men, raise storms and inflict illnesses and heal, and the like, he answered that he does not believe in anything of the said things nor in similar things.

Interrogated, then, whether the said friars burn witches rightly, he answered that he does not know whether it is fair or unfair, since one can err likewise in one sense or in the other.

Interrogated whether he believes that witches and sorcerers exist, he answered that he does not know, and that he does not really believe that sorcerers exist.

Interrogated whether he knows of anyone who calls him a witch, he said no.

Interrogated whether he himself ever said to be a witch, he said no.

Interrogated whether he ever invited someone to go to the sabbat, he answered that once this year he had said jokingly to a certain Andreino de la Tajada, from Maranello, these words, "Do you go to the sabbat?" And the said Andreino had said no. Brighento then had replied, "You will go there, too!" At that point Andreino had gone away insulting the said Brighento. (...)

Interrogated whether he ever said to any sick person that the cause of his/her illness had been to see some shadow or light, he answered that once, as he had been called by a certain lady called Grana, from Spezzano, the said Grana told Brighento that she had seen a man, and the mother-in-law of the said Grana [said] that it had been Grana's own shadow, and the said Brighento had then said that maybe that was someone returning from Sassuolo's fair.

Interrogated whether he ever went at night-time with a lamp, or without, he answered he never went, neither with a lamp nor without.

Interrogated whether he ever healed any men or animals, he answered he treats and [heals humans and animals], and among others, he healed a daughter of Facino from Sassuolo, and a certain Niccolò Pinelli, from Formiggine.

Interrogated specifically whether he treated a certain Jacopo de Gherardi, from Maranello, he answered yes, that is, with tow, which he had Jacopo put over his own head, because he suffered from "disce-sani."[2] (...)

Interrogated whether he ever signed the aforementioned Grana, or Jacopo, or anyone else, he answered no, except for the fact that he signs those suffering from hernia reciting the following prayer: "When Jesus Christ ascended to heaven/ Heaven and earth were shaken/ He met the Jewish dogs/ And they said, 'I am not shaking nor can I shake: I have hernia on me.' /(Jesus) said, 'Blessed be he who will believe me/ He will never have hernia.'/ In the name of the Father, of the Son and of the Holy Ghost."

Interrogated from whom did he learn this prayer, he answered from the aforementioned physician. (...)

Interrogated whether he ever asked anything from anyone for certain candles, he answered that he used to ask six "soldi" [type of coin] for his work ... which he spends on six candles, and he lights them to the image of the Glorious Virgin on whatever night and day, and while the candles burn and melt he remains kneeling because of a vow which he made for the plague, and he recites several Our Fathers and Hail Marys. (...)

(...)

[She testified that] last summer, around St. Peter's feast, as a certain Scontra Montanari had died, and she was returning home from his funeral at around one hour of night, although she feared nothing nor was she frightened by anything, she was attacked by a pain in a knee, and thus fell ill and remained ill for about seven months.

From that illness she became thin and dried up like a piece of wood, and she does not know, nor has found anybody who knows, what is her illness, except the said Brighento, who said that she had passed and trampled over an evil shadow. And the same witness, wishing to get better, called a doctor to cure her, who did her some oiling, after which she got worse. (...) Finally a doctor from the town of Sassuolo told her that she had been bewitched and had no more blood in her body, and that she had to go to a sorcerer because maybe she could be released by a sorcerer.

Thus the same witness went to Brighento, as he was someone with a widespread reputation for being a sorcerer; and he took on her treatment and finally healed her.

[She said] that she once asked the said Brighento why he did not heal her, and he answered, "You are going around joking about and slandering my ability." And as she was denying this, he replied, "I know what you say better than you do." And up until then she had never felt better, and had given him no money.

Interrogated, she said that after she had given money to the same Brighento, and saw she had gotten better following that, she started to speak ill of the said Brighento, since she suspected that he had bewitched her and waited to heal her so that he could gain something from her.

Interrogated about [Brighento's] healing method, she said that once she had decided that she wanted to ask the said Brighento for a cure, she went alone to his house, and asked him three times, for God's sake, to release her. She asked, or begged, him three times for God's sake because she had been forewarned that this is necessary with the said Brighento. And although he'd reproach her saying that there are so many tedious women, and that he would not cure her unless he wanted to, nevertheless he took on her treatment.

He told her that it was necessary that, as they say colloquially, "he would do it three times," on Sunday, Thursday, and Saturday, at night, and that she had to go to him on those days. As the same witness was suffering badly because of the swelling of the knee, the said Brighento said, "I will charm it." And thus, while he was kneeling, he charmed her swollen knee making some gestures with his hands.

In the following two days, the said witness saw the swelling diminish. (...) She eventually returned to Brighento, following his instructions ... and brought him seven "soldi," that he said he wanted for the candles he used. Thus the said Brighento signed the said knee and sent her back home, and told her that he would do it again ..., and that she had to keep a lighted lamp in her room during the night. She was thus signed three times, and she kept the lamp lit for three times.

Adding also that the aforementioned Brighento ordered her not to work if she wanted to be healed, and since she would not stop working, against Brighento's orders, it was necessary to restart the process and do everything all over again three times ... and the said witness was healed when, as the said Brighento affirmed, she had followed the rules in every detail, especially the rule of not working. (...)

Brighento was found by the inquisitor to be "lightly suspect" of the "heresy of the witches." He then recited the formula of abjuration, affirming solemnly that "Jesus Christ detests the heresy of the witches" and that those guilty of teaching it will burn eternally in Hell. He was forbidden to cure with superstitious systems and to praise or teach witchcraft, and he promised to present himself on every feast day to his parish priest in Maranello or to the inquisitor in Modena. He was also condemned to pay his trial's expenses.

Notes

1. This and all following passages between double quotation marks are in the Modenese vernacular in the original.

2. An unidentified disease.

A Witch at the Sabbat: Orsolina "la Rossa"[1]

Deposition and torture of Orsolina, 14 May 1539

This is a trial against Orsolina nicknamed la Rossa, wife of the late Pellegrino from Sassorosso, held against her by the inquisitor of the heretical depravity. She has first confessed to the reverend Don Ercole Montecuccoli, secular priest, prothonotary apostolical, and deputy commissar on heretical depravity.[2]

First interrogated whether she used to go to the ride, that is, to the sabbat, she answered yes.

Interrogated how long she has been going to the said ride, she answered she has been for the past forty years or circa.

Interrogated what does she do when she goes or wants to go to the said ride, or else sabbat, she answered: "I take some grease from my box and I grease a stick of crab-grass and I say 'Over leaf and under wind, beyond the sea there's the parley where I too want to go.'"

Interrogated what is that grease made of, she answered it is made from pork and duck fat.

Hearing these things, the aforementioned deputy commissar, knowing from her daughter Agnese's hearing[3] that she was a liar and was not telling the simple truth, ordered the said Orsolina to be tied up and brought near the fire, and had live charcoal put to her feet. As she felt the charcoal's heat, she said, "Take the fire away, since I want to tell the truth." (...)

As she was untied, she said these things: "I take my unguent, and I grease the palms of my hands, the waist and the neck, then I grease the stick and I conjure the devil like this: 'I deny Christ and the Virgin Mary and his saints, and I do not want God and the Virgin Mary to have anything to do with me nor with my soul, and may the devil be at my mercy and may I dominate him.' At his point I hit the ground with the stick, calling the devil three times like this, 'Devil, come for me.' At this point the devil will appear in the shape of a ram, and I ride him to the sabbat, where I find many sorcerers under the shade of a walnut tree. The said grease is made of human fat, olive tree leaves, and walnut wood ( ) charcoal."

Interrogated by the said apostolic commissar as to what she does at the said sabbat, she answered: "I go riding a ram as soon as ( ) and when I arrive there I find many other sorcerers and we eat oxen and dance together, then we have sexual intercourse with the devil indecently and in all possible ways." (...)

Interrogated who gave her that unguent or whether she herself made it, she said she did not make it but got it from a woman called Domenica Torrisella, who also goes to the sabbat, and added, "She also gave me some human fat, and so did Polo, an executioner from the village of Sassorosso."

Interrogated in what way she harms babies, she answered: "I suck their blood from under the nails of their hands or of their feet, or else from their lips, and I spit that blood into the hearth, after having first put all the ashes to the side, and I make a focaccia with that congealed blood and then I keep it. And if I were to find unguarded babies, woe to them!"

Orsolina retracts her confession, 10 June 1539

The aforementioned Orsolina was taken to Ferrara on orders from His Excellency the Duke [of Ferrara], and appeared before the inquisitor.

Interrogated whether she is Orsolina nicknamed La Rossa, detained and tried by the Reverend Don Ercole of Montecuccolo, Prothonotary and deputy of the Reverend inquisitor of Modena, she answered she is.

Interrogated whether the things she confessed to Don Ercole of Montecuccolo are true, she answered they are not. (...)

The inquisitor consults the bishop, 11 June 1539

The said inquisitor, seeing how obstinate and stubborn is the said Orsolina, went to the most reverend Monsignor of Castel Bolognese,[4] bishop of San Leone and suffragan bishop of Ferrara on behalf of the most reverend Monsignor Giovanni Salviati, cardinal deacon of the Saints Cosmas and Damian and bishop of Ferrara. He talked to him about the trial of the said Orsolina and asked him whether His Most Reverend Lordship wanted to be present at the interrogation under torture of the aforementioned defendant, and to use the authority of his office. The most reverend bishop judged the defendant to be examined under torture, and since he could not personally attend because of legitimate impediments, he delegated his authority to the said inquisitor, in the presence of witnesses.[5]

Summoned before the inquisitor, Orsolina swore and was admonished to tell the truth, whether the things written above in her trial are true or false. She answered she did truly confess all those things, nevertheless they are all false, and she does not want to confess anything anymore. (...)

Taken to the place of torture and interrogated whether she confesses the truth, she answered, "Do not torture me, I will tell the truth."

Interrogated whether she ever went to the sabbat, and for how long, she said she has been going for the past sixteen years.

Interrogated how many times she went, [she said] three times. (...)

Interrogated what did she see there the first time, she answered she saw a great crowd of men and women who jumped and ate and drank, and had goose feet. (...)

Interrogated where that was, she answered that the place she went to is a meadow near Coscogno, colloquially called the meadow of Coscogno, which is thirty miles away from Orsolina's house and near the castle called Sant'Almasso.

Interrogated what did she do there, she answered she did nothing, but only watched. (...)

Led then to the torture room, she was raised one ell above the ground and she said, "Put me down, and I will tell the truth."[6] Having been put down, she answered: "I used to go to the sabbat and denied the faith and the Virgin Mary, and I used to invoke the devil three times. He would come in the shape of a ram, and I would ride him as fast as the wind to a place called the Cross of the Oak."

She was then led to the torture room for the second time since she had not confessed the truth, and was raised one ell above the ground.

Interrogated whether she ever used a consecrated host to evil ends, she answered that only once she got a consecrated host from a certain Don Matteo from Monfestino, with whom she had dealings due to the spells that the said priest used to cast.

Interrogated what did she do with that consecrated host, she answered she gave it to her daughter.

Interrogated whether she cast spells on other children, she answered she had cast spells on three children, and that no one had died. (...)

Interrogated how long did she keep going to the sabbat, she answered once a week for three years in a row.

At this point, after Orsolina had been lifted above the ground for one quarter of a hour, the inquisitor ordered that the rope be jerked. Orsolina said, "Put me down, I will tell the truth."

Put down and interrogated whether she denied the faith when she went to the sabbat, she answered she denied the faith, God and and the Blessed Virgin Mary, and she gave herself over to the devil. The devil used to appear to her in the shape of a ram after having been conjured three times, and she rode him to the said place. (...)

Deposition and torture of Orsolina, 13 June 1539

The said Orsolina was led before the said reverend vicar [of the inquisition] and swore to tell the truth.

First of all, the aforementioned vicar recapitulated to her in the vernacular all the things she has confessed in the previous examination, and especially how she went to the sabbat seven times, and each time she denied God, Christ and His Mother, and invoked the devil, who appeared to her bodily and she gave herself over to him, and was then physically taken by him to the sabbat. There she worshiped the devil and had intercourse with him front and behind at once, and that happened always when she went to the sabbat. (...)

Interrogated under what guise did [the devil] appear to her at the sabbat when they had intercourse, she answered that he appeared as a handsome youth dressed in red.

Interrogated whether when she had intercourse with the devil she felt as if she was actually having intercourse with a real man, she answered yes, and that she has as much pleasure as if she were with a real man, and by the touch there is truly no difference from a real man.

Interrogated whether she knows that this is the devil, and from what sign she knows it, she answered that most certainly she knows that this is the devil, since he looks like a man from every respect but for the feet, which are round like those of a donkey. This is a feature that the devil wants to keep so that all those that sin by worshipping him will know that they really have sinned with the devil. (...)

Interrogated whether [she goes to the sabbat] always corporeally or rather in her dreams, she answered that there are many who only go in a vision, even though it is possible to also go corporeally, and she said that she always went corporeally.

Interrogated how does she know that she actually goes there corporeally, she answered that she would always go around sunset, before going to sleep, together with the other witches, all dressed as they had been during the day.

Interrogated whether anyone could go to the sabbat without denying the faith, she answered no.

Interrogated why so many men and women go to the sabbat and do not give up this vice, she answered that it is because of the extraordinary carnal pleasure they take with the devil, both men and women, and for no other reason than that. (...)

Deposition of Orsolina, 15 June 1539

(...)

Further, the said Orsolina, summoned [before the inquisitor], having sworn to tell the truth, interrogated whether those things she had confessed in the previous examinations were true, answered they were. (...)

Interrogated how was it possible to draw blood from babies' fingers by sucking, as she has confessed, she answered that under both the thumb and the big toe there is a certain big vein, and that if they [the witches] pierce the finger or toe near that vein with either their nails or some other tool, they can draw as much blood as they want. She also says that babies often cry because of such a wound, and therefore if they are guarded witches must run away.

Further, ordered to continue to confess her crimes as she had begun to do in the previous examination, and interrogated how she could know for sure that she would actually go bodily to the sabbat, she answered that she would know it due to two reasons: first, sometimes she would leave [for the sabbat] before going to sleep; second, because her husband once noticed that she was not in bed nor in the house, waited for her to return, and gave her a good thrashing.

Further, she said that once about fourteen witches, lead by the devil who opened the door, entered a house in a place called Mesola, near Mocogno, and took away a babe, whose parents she does not know. They first sucked his blood, then they beat him heavily with a stick, so that he died, then they cut him to pieces and ate him, though she says she did not eat anything from his flesh but only drank part of his blood. She also said that someone from that house, realizing the baby was not there anymore, ran after the said witches. (...)

Interrogated why she did not kill more people than those she had confessed, she answered she would have killed many more had she had the chance, but often parents would wake up and chase them [the witches], and they would run away in fear. Anyway, all those babies they would find unguarded when going to the sabbat, they would either kill or bewitch.

Orsolina was found guilty of heresy, and on 28 October 1539 Friar Tommaso of Morbegno, vicar general and commissar of the Inquisition in Modena, condemned her to house arrest for life, with the only exception of attending mass. She was also condemned to wear visibly for a year a special garment with a red cross, to recite every day of her life the rosary of the Virgin (that is, fifteen Our Fathers and one hundred Hail Marys), and to stay kneeling at the door of Modena's cathedral four feast days in a row with a rope at her neck, telling everybody, "I am here to atone for my sins, since I have been a heretic, a witch and a sorceress and I have scandalized my neighbor."

Notes

1. Contrary to all previous documents, this trial's transcripts are mostly in the vernacular.

2. Ercole Montecuccoli, from an old family of powerful and fearsome counts, was the vicar of the Inquisition in the village of Gaiato, 3,000 feet high at the heart of his family's fiefs, in the Frignano area of the Appennines (about thirty miles south-west of Modena). The Modenese Inquisition did not have sufficient resources to keep direct control over such a remote area of the state, the more so since the Frignano had a strong tradition of rebelliousness to outside powers. This is why Tommaso of Morbegno, then inquisitor of Modena, had to rely on a local secular priest such as Montecuccoli as his commissar, instead of having one of his fellow Dominicans try the witch. The first part of Orsolina's trial took place in Gaiato, and most of the places mentioned by her in the examinations are located within a ten-mile radius of the village. The role of Montecuccoli likely accounts for at least one of the peculiarities of this trial, namely the recourse to fire as a means of torture, rarely used by the Inquisition at this time (and practically unheard-of in Modena).

3. Agnese was tried for witchcraft by the Modenese Inquisition in the same weeks as her mother.

4. Ottaviano of Castel Bolognese, suffragan bishop of Ferrara during 1535-42.

5. Ottaviano had to delegate his authority to the inquisitor because in his absence the inquisitor could not have proceeded against Orsolina, since canon law decreed that no heretic could be tortured or sentenced to any pain without the local bishop's approval.

6. This was the torture system called strappado ("la corda" in Italian, literally "the rope"), the one most commonly used by inquisitors in the peninsula (Fig. 2). The defendant's hands were tied behind her or his back and tied to a rope which, through a pulley, raised him or her several feet above the ground. The defendant was then interrogated while in this position. If a confession was not obtained thus, the inquisitor would sometimes command the rope to be jerked to increase the level of pain (for the same purpose he could have weights tied to the defendant's ankles).

ENDNOTES

Notes to the Introduction

1. The "Inquisition" as a centralized and unified court system, in reality, did not come into being until the mid-sixteenth century as far as the Italian peninsula is concerned. For the previous centuries it would be thus more precise to speak of individual "inquisitors," but for the sake of simplicity I have preferred to use the term "Inquisition" in all cases since it conflates the judicial functions carried out by regular clergy (Dominican and Franciscan friars) and the ideological profile of their activity within the overall papal effort to fight religious dissent and witchcraft. See below, pp. 22ff.

2. The best one-volume presentation of the history of the witch-hunts is Levack 2006. Briggs 1996 provides both new insights and a balanced discussion of earlier scholarship on the social context of the witch-hunts. See also Waite 2003, Behringer 2004. Ankarloo and Clark 2002 (6 volumes) is the most complete historical survey of the topic, while Golden 2006 (4 volumes) provides accessible and reliable scholarly reference on all aspects of witchcraft and witch-hunts.

3. The present book will not address the issue of Renaissance learned magic at any length, since it lies outside of its scope. Bibliography on this theme is very vast: for a first orientation see Clark 2002, 147-69.

Notes to Chapter One

1. Peters 1978, 91-98; and Kieckhefer 2000, 181-86; see a selection of Aquinas' writings on sorcery (in English translation) in Kors and Peters 2001, 87-105.

2. See the text in Kors and Peters 2001, 127-32; Peters 2002, 207-17.

3. Levack 2006, 88-95; and Peters 2002, 213-18, 234.

4. On both civil and ecclesiastical law on magic and witchcraft, see Peters 1978, especially 148-55.

5. The text, and its complex tradition, in Kors and Peters 2001, 60-63, 72-73. On *Episcopi* and its importance for the debate on witchcraft see below, p. 19.

6. Levack 2006, 75-80; and Peters 2002, 207-25.

7. Levack 2006, 80-88.

8. See below, pp. 22ff.

9. Kors and Peters 2001, 120-27. But see below, pp. 47-48, for a narrower interpretation of this principle by Modena's inquisitors, resulting in a usually lenient treatment of magicians.

10. Peters 1978, 152-54.

11. A selection of the most important volumes on the origins of the witch-hunts published in English in the last thirty years includes Cohn 1975; Kieckhefer 1976; Peters 1978; Ginzburg 1983; and idem 1991; Waite 2003 is an up-to-date general presentation of the issue from a religious history angle (with extensive bibliography). Macfarlane 1970 and Thomas 1971 are pioneering and largely influential studies on the social origins of the witch-hunts and their cultural genesis in England.

12. Peters 2002, 223-37.

13. Ostorero 1999 is an important edition of the earliest texts on witchcraft (in their original languages with French translation). See a selection from the books by Nider, Jacquier and Tholosan, in English translation, in Kors and Peters 2001, 155-59, 169-72, 162-66, which also contains other texts from this period. A selection from these and other works from the same period, in Italian translation, in Abbiati 1984, 52-99. Bailey 2003 is a study on this early phase of demonology and especially on Nider.

14. Clark 1997 is a comprehensive, fundamental study of witchcraft theories. Thomas 1971 discusses also close beliefs—magic, astrology etc.—and is still very important, especially for England. The definition of a "cumulative theory" of witchcraft is first given in Russell 1972, 34, and clarified in Levack 2006, 29ff.

15. Stephens 2002, 58-86, 125-44.

16. Kors and Peters 2001, 133-37.

17. Kors and Peters 2001, 152-55, 177-80.

18. More precisely, these territories include present-day Savoy (France) and Valle d'Aosta (Italy), and the towns and territories of Lausanne, Neuchâtel, Basel, Bern, Fribourg, Lucerne, and the Valais (Switzerland). The relevant scholarship is summarized in Peters 2002, 233-45. Behringer 2004, 60ff., provides the best account and analysis of the early phase of the witch-hunts.

19. See Levack 2006, especially 204-32 for chronology and geography of the hunts.

20. See Broedel 2003; Behringer 2006. Krämer 1971, a well-known but largely defective modern edition of the *Malleus Maleficarum* in English translation, is now surpassed by the much more careful and reliable (although abridged) Krämer 2007, likewise in English; a selection from the Krämer 1971 edition in Kors and Peters 2001, 180-229. It is worth adding that another Dominican, Jacob Sprenger (to whom, along with Krämer, Pope Innocent VIII had addressed the 1484 "Witch-Bull"), has traditionally been indicated as the co-author of the book; however, historians have dismissed this attribution as unfounded.

21. On Krämer's inquisitorial activity, see Waite 2003; and Herzig 2006.

22. Levack 2006, 141ff. The "gendering" of witchcraft has attracted considerable scholarly attention, and bibliography on the topic is very vast: see Wiesner 1993; Briggs 1996; Roper 1994; and idem 2004.

23. Kors and Peters 2001, 60-63, 72-73.

24. On Diana's retinue, variously referred to in pre-modern Europe as the "wild hunt," or the "furious horde," see Ginzburg 1983, 40-50.

25. On Nider, see Bailey 2003; on Alphonso de Spina, see Lea 1957 1:285-92; and Maxwell-Stuart 2006.

26. On Becchi, see Thorndike 1923-58, 4:698-99.

27. On Vignati, see Lea 1957, 1:299-301; and Bonomo 1985, 374-77. On Molitor, see Bever 2006.

28. On Cassini, see Valente 2006a.

29. On Ponzinibio and Spina, see Vanysacker 2006; and Zarri 2006, respectively.

30. On Alciato, or Alciati, see Duni 2006a.

31. On Cardano and Weyer, see Ernst 2006; and Valente 2006b, respectively.

32. See the relevant entries in Golden 2006.

33. Peters 1989, 40-74.

34. Kieckhefer 1995; Peters 1989, 67-71; and Dinzelbacher 2006.

35. Bibliography on the early modern Inquisitions is very vast: good starting points are Peters 1989 and Bethencourt 1995; the entries on the Portuguese, Roman and Spanish Inquisitions in Golden 2006 are also a useful first reference. Del Col 2006 is a comprehensive history of the Inquisition in the Italian peninsula, from its origin to its contemporary version; it was published too late to be taken into account in this book. Romeo 2006 focuses on the Roman Inquisition in the early modern period. The *Dizionario storico dell'Inquisizione* edited by Adriano Prosperi, to be published in Italian in 2008, will be the new standard reference work on all issues related to the Inquisition in its different forms and epochs.

36. Kieckhefer 1995; and Bethencourt 1995, 35-36. For Modena, Duni 1999, 19; and Tedeschi 1991, 130, albeit mostly in reference to the later Roman Inquisition.

37. Tedeschi 1991, 142 (in this case also valid for the medieval Inquisition).

38. Tedeschi 1991, 143.

39. Peters 1989, 59-67. Bethencourt 1995 is a thorough comparative analysis of all procedures of the early modern Inquisitions. It is worth adding, however, that in the Italian peninsula procedures underwent significant changes following the institution of the Roman Inquisition during the later part of the sixteenth century (see below, pp. 31ff).

40. Tedeschi 1991, 135-40.

41. Tedeschi 1991, 141-47; and Peters 1989, 65.

42. Levack 2006, 85.

43. Tedeschi 1991, 144-45.

44. Peters 1989, 67.

45. Ibid.

46. Housley 1982; and Terpstra 1996.

47. There is anyway an excellent starting point, the useful and generally accurate calendar of witch-trials in Europe during 1300-1500, in Kieckhefer 1976, 106-47; for the sixteenth century see Lea 1957, 1:242ff.; see also Di Simplicio 2006.

48. Peters 1978, 129-35; and Peters 2002, 212-14.

49. Kors and Peters 2001, 116-18.

50. Kors and Peters 2001, 119-20.

51. Peters 1978, 105-106.

52. See Biondi 1993, who includes an Italian translation of Benvenuta's trial on 101-24.

53. Kieckhefer 1976, 21-22; and Muraro 1976, 147-55 (see there also the text of the sentence against Sibillia and Pierina—in the original Latin—on 240-45); on the female goddess who resurrects eaten animals, see Bertolotti 1991.

54. See a selection of trials, in English translation, in Brucker 1971, 260-73.

55. See the original Latin text of the trial of Matteuccia di Francesco and its English translation (both with numerous mistakes) in Mammoli 1972; and Monter 2006. Vehement anti-witchcraft sermons delivered in Todi's area by Franciscan Bernardino of Siena in the previous years may have been connected to Matteuccia's subsequent trial: see Mormando 1999, 72-80.

56. Kieckhefer 1976, 122-30. The Val Leventina is a valley that was part of the duchy of Milan and is now part of the Swiss Canton Ticino.

57. An exception in this picture was represented by the Valle d'Aosta, ruled by the Savoy dukes in the extreme northwest of the Italian peninsula, where Franciscan inquisitors reached a peak of activity in the repression of witchcraft precisely during the 1440s (Bertolin and Gerbore 2003). It is true, however, that in this respect the Valle d'Aosta was following the intense witch-hunting trend prevalent in the neighboring French-speaking Alpine regions, such as the Pays de Vaud, likewise under Savoy rule.

58. Mormando 1999, 52-72.

59. Kieckhefer 1976, 142, with the relevant references to the *Malleus Maleficarum* (Krämer 1971, 66, 99, 111, 230). The information given by the *Malleus* is confirmed by other local sources: see Bonomo 1985, 141-43, 253-54 (see also in Bonomo 1985, chap. 7, a chronology—not entirely reliable—of early witchcraft trials in Italy).

60. Prosperi 1996, 386-88; and Bonomo 1985, 141-43.

61. Lea 1957, 1:374-76; and Duni 2006a.

62. The actual trials are lost, but a substantial body of Venetian government papers, official correspondence and personal diaries permits a fairly accurate reconstruction of the events: see Del Col 1988, 250-59; and Bonomo 1985, 94, 281, 302-03.

63. See the transcripts of these trials in the original Latin with facing Italian translation in Marcaccioli Castiglioni 1999.

64. The witch-hunt of Mirandola has attracted considerable scholarly attention (even though the trials' papers are lost): see Burke 1977; Biondi 1989; Stephens 2002, 87-99; and Pico della Mirandola 2007.

65. Pico della Mirandola 2007 is the new critical edition of *Strix* (in French translation); see also an annotated edition of the Italian text in Pico della Mirandola 1989.

66. Levack 2006, 205-206, after mentioning some of the witch-hunts in the Italian peninsula (and elsewhere) during the first decades of the sixteenth century, states that this was "a period of relative tranquility as far as witchcraft was concerned;" clearly this judgment requires qualification in the light of the conclusions reached so far. See Behringer 2004, 77-79.

67. For Venice, see Del Col 1988, 247-50 (discussing also cases tried by the court of the Patriarch of Venice); for Modena, see Biondi 1977; and Duni 1999, 28-33.

68. See a selection from Orsolina's trial in the Appendix, pp. 115-21; part of the trial transcript (in the original Italian) was published in Romanello 1975, 119-31.

69. For a first orientation on the impact of the Protestant Reformation in Italy, see Cameron 1992; an invaluable guide to the very vast bibliography on this topic is Tedeschi 2000.

70. A brief survey in Peters 1989, 105-21; Tedeschi 1991 is a collection of fundamental studies on the topic; of great importance in connection with magic and witchcraft Romeo 1990; and Prosperi 1996, 368-430. The opening of the central archives of the Holy Office in the Vatican in 1998 will very likely modify the landscape of our knowledge of the tribunal in the future: Romeo 2006 (3rd edition) is the first synthesis produced after the opening; see also Del Col 2006.

71. Monter and Tedeschi 1986, 133-34 (reprinted in Tedeschi 1991, 89-126). See also the figures, and the cautionary note, in Romeo 1990,

177-79, whose findings, anyway, go in the same direction.

72. See Duni 1999, 28-33; and Trenti 2003, 49-58 (this is a general analytical inventory of the inquisitorial archives in Modena from 1489 to the tribunal's suppression in 1784, which gives a classification by type of crime of the cases dealt with by the Modenese Inquisition); Duni 2006b.

73. A selection of introductory texts in English to the history of the Counter Reformation and its impact on religious life includes Delumeau 1977, and Hsia 2005. For Italy, see Prosperi 1996.

74. Romeo 1990, especially 169-246; and Prosperi 1996, 389-98.

75. Monter and Tedeschi 1986, 144; and Martin 1989, 216.

76. As a matter of fact, exactly half of the eighty-eight cases over the period 1581-1600 occurred during the year 1600 alone (these figures are drawn, with minor corrections and adjustments, from Trenti 2003, 49-54). One major political and institutional change helps explain the skyrocketing figures of the last years of the century: in 1598 Modena became the capital city of the duchy ruled by the Este house, and consequently also the seat of an inquisitor general who had a wider jurisdiction than the vicars of the previous period (although not over the entire state) and was likely provided with more substantial resources to carry out his tasks.

77. Prosperi 1996, 373-77; and Romeo 1990, 48-52 (see there n. 50 on 44-45 for a survey of death sentences for witchcraft in the peninsula during the last decades of the century).

78. The witch-hunt in Triora was anomalous in various respects. Trials were conducted by several different judges both secular and ecclesiastical, dozens of suspects were interrogated and jailed—and several of them died in custody—but apparently no witch was ever sent to the stake. The episode still lacks a comprehensive scholarly reconstruction, also because the surviving documentation has serious gaps. See Coppo and Panizza 1990.

79. Tedeschi 1990; and Romeo 1990, 25-65; but see more recently Dall'Olio 2001; and Lavenia 2001, who, also thanks to documents now accessible after the opening of the Holy Office's central archives, are able to show that such a cautious approach was already present (although not prevalent) within the Roman Inquisition's top board as early as 1559.

80. See above, pp. 20-21.

81. Romeo 1990, 67-70, 85-92.

82. See Prosperi 1996, 57-116; and Lavenia 2001, 39-40 and passim.

83. Romeo 1990, 86ff.; and Kallestrup 2006.

84. See Tedeschi 1991, 205-27, who dates the *Instructio* around 1624; recent research, however, indicates an earlier date as likely for the composition of this document: see Decker 1998.

85. See O'Neil 1984; idem 1987; Romeo 1990, 201-46; and Gentilcore 1992, 95-122.

86. O'Neil 1987; more in general Prosperi 1996, 230ff. on the establishment of the obligation for the confessors in cases of heresy.

87. O'Neil 1984; Gentilcore 1992; and Prosperi 1996, 418-30.

Notes to Chapter Two

1. See Ginzburg 1989, and the critical remarks in Del Col 2000.

2. At least in the Modenese cases, as a matter of fact, love magic was most often meant to be an attack on a person's health, with the aim of making his or her will give in to another person's attraction.

3. On the theme of the communication and reciprocal influence between "high" and "low" culture see Ginzburg 1980; idem 1986; and Gentilcore 1992, 1-17.

4. Martin 1989, 192.

5. *Inquisizione*, busta 2, fasc. I, deposition of Beatrice Falloppia, 15 January 1499. This and all following quotes from Inquisition documents come from the series *Inquisizione* in the State Archives of Modena. I have used double quotation marks to indicate the original headings of the trials when present.

6. Ginzburg 1983 analyzes in depth pre-Christian agrarian roots of the sabbat's image.

7. *Inquisizione*, busta 2, fasc. II, "Against Zilia," deposition of Giovanni da Ronco, 23 February 1519.

8. Bertolotti 1991.

9. See above, p. 27.

10. Bertolotti 1991; Ginzburg 1990; and Duni 1999, 37-39.

11. Duni 2006b; the complete inventory of the (now lost) trials conducted by the Inquisition of nearby Reggio Emilia shows that witch-hunting in that area reached its climax likewise in the decade between the mid-1520s and the late 1530s (see Romeo 1990, 53-54), also due to the witch-hunt of Mirandola (on which see above, p. 30).

12. *Inquisizione*, busta 2, fasc. III, "Against Orsolina nicknamed la Rossa." See a selection from her trial in the Appendix, pp. 115-21.

13. Tommasino de' Bianchi, or else de' Lancellotti (1473-1554), was a wealthy Modenese notary and banker who recorded events of the most diverse kind in his twelve-volume *Cronicha* (chronicle), a wonderfully vivid and detailed description of Modena's people and their history from 1506 to 1554. See Orsolina's auto-da-fè (in Italian) in Bianchi 1862-84, VI:230.

14. Thus Orsolina was not "the only witch ever sentenced to death in Modena," as I erroneously wrote in Duni 2006b. Indeed, it is likely that *no* witch was sent to the stake in Modena, at least as far as the sixteenth century is concerned.

15. *Inquisizione*, busta 3, fasc. VI. On her trial, see Romeo 1990, 54-59.

16. Antonia had been condemned by Campeggi's vicar in Modena, Friar Vincenzo of Imola, to undergo public shaming rituals for several Sundays in a row, and to exile from Modena for life.

17. See Biondi 1982 on the organization of the tribunal.

18. On necromancy, its literature, sources and practice, see Kieckhefer 2000, 151-75; and idem 1998, who analyzes in depth one manual of necromancy.

19. The best study on the *Clavicula Salomonis*, its very complex tradition, and on the various uses of this and similar works by early modern magicians, is Barbierato 2002, who focuses on seventeenth- and eighteenth-century Venice. A modern edition of the *Clavicula* in English translation is Liddel MacGregor Mathers 1889, not always reliable. See also Kieckhefer 1998.

20. Kieckhefer 2000, 159-65.

21. Biondi 1993, 104.

22. *Inquisizione*, busta 2, "Against Francesco de Ottono," deposition of Gabriele da Salò, 16 July 1498.

23. *Inquisizione*, busta 2, "Complete Trial against Don Guglielmo Campana," (henceforth referred to as "Against Don Campana"), depositions of Don Campana, 17 January and 12 March 1517. See Appendix, pp. 83-86, 87-88.

24. Ginzburg 1970. See Appendix, p. 100.

25. *Inquisizione*, busta 2, deposition of Bernardina Stadera, 2 December 1499. See Appendix, pp. 78-80.

26. Peters 1978, 96-98; and Martin 1989, 148-74, who examines the—very similar—approach of the Venetian Inquisition to various types of magic.

27. Thomas 1971, 25-50.

28. It must be noted, however, that from a theological point of view a difference existed between sacraments and sacramentals, as the former (which numbered seven) were supposed to be always valid if the rite was correctly performed by a duly ordained minister, independently of his worthiness. However, the efficacy of the sacramentals (a variable number, including sign of the cross, litanies, rosary, exorcism, etc.), was thought to rest on the Church's intercession and not on the performance of the rite alone, and to be influenced by the performer's moral and religious disposition (see Cross and Livingstone 1988, s.v. "sacrament," "sacramental"). Furthermore, theologians stressed that all Church rituals had first of all spiritual effects, that could eventually produce positive material consequences; but of course the subtlety of official doctrine was largely lost on the majority of the faithful.

29. Gentilcore 1992, 15-17.

30. For the issue of the lower clergy's culture and inability to respect the—often vague—boundaries between orthodoxy and superstition, see O'Neil 1984, passim; Gentilcore 1992, chaps. 2 and 4, is an excellent analysis of the social and cultural world of the lower clergy in southern Italy during the early modern period.

31. See the letter of William Cardinal of Santa Sabina, issued in 1320 on behalf of Pope John XXII to the inquisitors of Carcassonne and Toulouse, denouncing those who perform demonic magic as guilty also of abusing sacraments, and calling the Inquisition to prosecute them (Kors and Peters 2001, 118-19); see also Martin 1989, 59ff. for the

impact of Eymeric's influential *Directorium Inquisitorum* (1376) on the Inquisition's view of sacramental abuses in magical practices.

32. One remarkable such case is that of the sorceress Anastasia "la Frappona," who was convicted also for abuses of baptism and of holy oil in 1519. See Appendix, pp. 102-03. On the other hand, in the first three decades of the sixteenth century no charge was ever brought against several clergymen that many witnesses indicated as abusing consecrated objects, and one has to wait for the last twenty years of the century to see an ecclesiastic condemned for such a crime.

33. See O'Neil 1987, 94.

34. Fantini 1996; and idem 1999; see Cohen and Cohen 1993, 189-99, for the use of the same prayer by a late sixteenth century Roman courtesan.

35. A litany is a form of prayer which begs the three persons of the Trinity, the Virgin Mary, a series of prophets, patriarchs, angels, apostles, and saints, to have mercy and bring deliverance to the congregation or the single faithful. See Cross and Livingstone 1988, s.v. "litany" and "litany of the saints."

36. *Inquisizione*, busta 2, fasc. II, "Against Costanza Barbetta," deposition of Laura Betocchia, 29 December 1518 (Appendix, p. 93). See Kieckhefer 1998, 133-34, for the analysis of invocations in magical formulas and a comparison with orthodox prayers.

37. *Inquisizione*, busta 2, fasc. II, "Against Anastasia la Frappona," deposition of Anastasia, 17 October 1519.

38. *Inquisizione*, busta 2, fasc. II, "Against Giulia of Bologna," deposition of Giulia, October 5, and her abjuration, 9 October 1518.

39. "Against Costanza Barbetta," deposition of Laura Betocchia, 28 December 1518; Appendix, p. 92.

40. "Against Giulia of Bologna," deposition of Elisabetta Dene, 21 December 1518. The use of animal parts, especially the heart, for love magic techniques was common: see for example the trial of the Florentine sorcerer Niccolò Consigli (1384) in Brucker 1971, 263; and the Modenese trial of Costanza Barbetta, who according to Laura Betocchia used the ashes from the heart of a hen to force Filippo Barbetta to love her ("Against Costanza Barbetta," deposition of Laura, 29 December 1518).

41. "Against Anastasia la Frappona," deposition of Anastasia, 11 October 1519.

42. *Inquisizione*, busta 2, fasc. II, "Against Baila," deposition of several witnesses, 11 April 1520.

43. Appendix, p. 102.

44. "Against Anastasia la Frappona," deposition of Alessandro Valentini, 20 September 1519.

45. See for instance "Against Anastasia la Frappona," deposition of 11 October 1519, Appendix, p. 98.

46. "Against Don Campana," depositions of Don Campana, 11 and 12 March 1517.

47. Duni 1999, 199-200. It is worth stressing that instructions to make wax images for maleficent purposes could be practically absent from certain versions of the *Clavicula*—such as the one used by Liddell MacGregor Mathers for the modern English edition—while figuring very prominently in others. Indeed, books of this kind could circulate in so great a variety of versions as to make their very identification extremely difficult (see Barbierato 2002).

48. *Inquisizione*, busta 2, fasc. I, deposition of Friar Giovanni of Modena, 20 November 1495.

49. *Inquisizione*, busta 2, deposition of Ludovico Bottacci, 26 May 1496.

50. "Against Don Campana," memorandum by Don Campana to the inquisitor, 5 April 1517.

51. On the powers attributed to demons, see Flint 1991, 146ff.; and especially Clark 1997, 161-78 and passim.

52. See Kieckhefer 1998, 125-49 for examples of such equivalence.

53. Thomas 1971, 234-37; Martin 1989, 87-92; Gentilcore 1992, 219, 230.

54. *Inquisizione*, busta 2, fasc. I, deposition of Friar Giovanni of Modena, 20 November 1495.

55. The Roman Ritual is the official service book of the Roman Rite, and includes the procedures for all Church rituals with the exception of the Mass.

56. "Against Don Campana," deposition of Don Campana, 22 January

1517. Appendix, p. 86.

57. Kieckhefer 1998, 96-125.

58. Kors and Peters 2001, 131.

59. Zuan delle Piatte was tried in 1501 and 1504 in the Val di Fiemme area of the Trentino region (see Kral 1995, 427); "Against Don Campana," deposition of Don Campana, 11 March 1517. See also Ginzburg 1983, 49-51, for an interesting case of scrying from Mantua at the end of the fifteenth century.

60. His name was Carlo Sosenna, and his "servant spirit" was so well-known as to be mentioned by Ludovico Ariosto, one of the most famous Renaissance poets, in one of his *Satires* (VII, 94-96; see Biondi 1977, 176-77).

61. *Inquisizione*, busta 2, fasc. I, "Against Francesco de Ottoni," deposition of Gabriele da Salò, 16 July 1498; ibid. "Against Bernardina Stadera," deposition of Giovanna Mascarelli, 8 December 1499, Appendix, pp. 78-79.

62. "Against Don Campana," deposition of Don Campana, 17 January 1517, Appendix, p. 83.

63. Appendix, p. 79.

64. On the recourse to children for fortune-telling practices—which dates back to Classical antiquity—see Thomas 1971, 255-56, 320; fundamental Grottanelli 1993.

65. Don Gugliemo used this technique to find stolen property ("Against Don Campana," deposition of Don Campana, 11 March 1517); see Martin 1989, 117, for a more complete version of the prayer as used by Venetian enchantresses.

66. On this important Bull, which condemned all forms of astrology and learned magic, see Thorndike 1959, VI:145-78; and Romeo 2006, 37-38.

67. "Against Anastasia la Frappona," deposition of Eleonora Mantovani, 24 January 1519, Appendix, p. 96.

68. Biondi 1993, 101-102.

69. On this very vast theme, see Ginzburg 1983; and idem 1991.

70. See Ruggiero 1993, 107-109 (the whole chapter is important for its

analysis of different magical techniques).

71. *Inquisizione*, busta 2, fasc. II, "Against Costanza Barbetta," deposition of Maria Burdini, 7 January 1519.

72. On the connection between quarrels and *maleficium*, and the search for explanations, Thomas 1971 (especially 502-69) and Macfarlane 1970 are fundamental; see more recently Briggs 1996, especially 63-95, for an analysis of the social context of witchcraft accusations.

73. *Inquisizione*, busta 2, fasc. II, "Against Chiara Signorini," deposition of Paolo Magnani, January 1519; on Chiara's trial, see Ginzburg 1990.

74. See Ginzburg 1983, 78; and Levack 2006, 11.

75. See Levack 2006, 160-61, on the tendency to accuse of witchcraft individuals who had a reputation for bad temper and polemical attitudes.

76. *Inquisizione*, busta 2, fasc. II, "Against Giulia of Bologna," deposition of Giuliana, nicknamed "la Negra," Tosetti, 17 February 1519.

77. "Against a woman called la Menigotta," depositions of Giovanni Antonio Gotti and Francesco Silingardi, 14 and 16 April 1520, respectively.

78. The belief that witches could harm children by sucking their blood is connected to the ancient myth of *strigae* (screech owls) that would eat infants, and to other classical and medieval legends: see Levack 2006, 45-50.

79. "Against Giulia of Bologna," deposition of Giovan Pietro de Coperti, 20 September 1519.

80. "Against Anastasia la Frappona," deposition of Maddalena Facchini, 14 October 1519. See Levack 2006, 5-7, who distinguishes on such grounds *maleficium* from sorcery.

81. See Martin 1989, 196.

82. *Inquisizione*, busta 2, fasc. II, "Against Giacoma de Bagarini," deposition of Eleonora, wife of Michele Antonio from Castellarano, 15 June 1519.

83. "Against Chiara Signorini," deposition of Paolo Magnani, January 1519.

84. Deposition of Chiara, 9 February 1519.

85. "Against Costanza Barbetta," deposition of Laura Betocchia, 28 December 1518; Appendix, pp. 92-93.

86. See the clarifying remarks by Ferber 2004, 115ff.

87. See Ferber 2004 and Romeo 1990, 117-22, discussing the works of the Franciscan Girolamo Menghi (1529-1609), famous exorcist who was convinced of the human origin of most demonic possessions.

88. See Piccinini 1997 for the most up-to-date discussion of the saint's cult in the middle ages and the early modern period.

89. "Against Don Campana," deposition of Lucrezia Pasini, 13 January 1517.

90. *Inquisizione*, busta 2, fasc. II, "Against Friar Bernardino and Don Guglielmo Campana," deposition of Giovanni Magnani, 30 December 1518. The name of Astaroth, "prince of the demons," was commonly listed in books of necromancy: see Kieckhefer 1998, 162.

91. See O'Neil 1984, 71-73; Duni 1999, 215-17.

92. On medical culture and practice of the times, see Park 1985 and Siraisi 1990.

93. See Schmitt 2001.

94. Gentilcore 1998, 1-28, 156-76 (the whole book is important for the theme of medical pluralism); Park 1998.

95. O'Neil 1984, especially 57-60; and Duni 1999, 167-70, 249-53.

96. Park 1998, especially 138-40; Biondi 1981; and Agrimi and Crisciani 1992.

97. Gentilcore 1998, 161-65.

98. "Against Don Campana," deposition of Pellegrina Guidotti, 4 January 1517.

99. Schmitt 2001.

100. Gentilcore 1992, 102-05; and O'Neil 1984, 60-61.

101. *Inquisizione*, busta 2, fasc. III, "Against Brighento Brighenti," deposition of Maddalena Ferrari, 3 March 1531; Appendix, p. 113.

102. Ruggiero 1993, 149-56, 163-66.

103. See Ruggiero 1993, 156-73, for many other examples of *histori-*

ole from trials of the Venetian Inquisition; Martin 1989, 144-47.

104. "Against Brighento Brighenti," deposition of Brighento, 25 February, 1531; Appendix, p. 112.

105. See De Martino 1966, 96-97, 104 for the logic of this mechanism. In recent years Ernesto De Martino's pioneering ethnological studies on the religious beliefs and practices of the lower classes of the Italian South have influenced historians working on the early modern period: see Gentilcore 1992.

106. "Against Don Campana," deposition of Don Campana, 17 January 1517; Appendix, p. 84. The sweetness of the milk of the Virgin Mary was frequently invoked by healers to counteract the bitterness of patients' sufferings.

107. The celebrated Florentine physician Antonio Benivieni in his *De Abditis Nonnullis ac Mirandis Morborum et Sanationum Causis (On Some Occult and Amazing Causes of Diseases and Cures*, 1502) records the case of a priest healed from toothache by a peasant who hammered a nail in the ground while reciting some formulas (Benivieni 1994, 176).

108. "Against Giulia of Bologna," deposition of Giuliana Tosetti, nicknamed "la Negra," 17 February 1519.

109. Not by chance, in the belief-complex studied in Ginzburg 1983 for the northern Italian region of Friuli, the "benandanti" (sort of anti-witches) were supposed to fight witches and warlocks using fennel stalks as weapons.

110. "Against Vincenzo of Reggio," deposition of Vincenzo, 1 January 1519.

111. See Martin 1989, 142-43.

112. See Russell 1972, 51, 248, also stressing that witches' meetings were believed by some to be held near Midsummer's Eve; Rivera 1988; Flint 1991, 315-17, remarks that St. John the Evangelist's feast (27 December), close to the winter solstice, was also considered an important moment for gathering medicinal herbs, like St. John's wort (it is worth adding that the faithful frequently confused the two saints).

113. "Against Costanza Barbetta," deposition of Laura Betocchia, 29 December 1518.

114. Against Don Campana," deposition of Don Campana, 17 January 1517, and list of Campana's crimes compiled by inquisitor: Appendix, pp. 85, 89.

115. Duni 1999, 264-70.

116. Measuring an ailing person's waist, or a sick baby's swaddlings, was a fairly common diagnostic technique with healers: see Ruggiero 1993, 153-55.

117. "Against Don Campana," deposition of Don Campana, 17 January 1517; Appendix, p. 85.

118. These and following figures are drawn, with minor modifications, from Trenti 2003, 49-64, who refers to folders 2-14 of the *Inquisizione* series of the State Archives of Modena.

119. O'Neil 1987, 101; Cohen and Cohen 1993, 189-99, for the case of Roman courtesans; see also Tedeschi 1991, 234-5, on the opinion that prostitutes were often involved in love magic.

120. See also O'Neil 1984, 56, whose total of prosecutions during 1580-1600 is however inaccurate.

121. See Duni 1999, especially 120-34, for the most dramatic case, that of Don Campana's trial, but also for the lesser one of Don Giovannino Carafoli (1519), 40-43.

122. Duni 1999, 175-82.

123. See Ruggiero 1993, 206-12, on a group of Venetian patricians interested in using demonic magic to find hidden treasures.

124. Appendix, pp. 111-12.

125. Appendix, pp. 107, 109.

126. See "Against Giulia of Bologna," deposition of Ludovico Dene, 19 February 1519; and "Against Costanza Barbetta," deposition of Laura Betocchia, 29 December 1518. On the Cimera's trial, judged by the inquisitor and demonologist Silvestro Mazzolini, see Tavuzzi 1997, 37.

127. On books of secrets, see Eamon 1994; and Park 1998.

128. *Inquisizione*, busta 8, fasc. I, "Against Friar Ippolito Scapinelli," 9 May 1589, deposition of Friar Ippolito.

129. O'Neil 1984; and Romeo 1990.

BIBLIOGRAPHY

Abbiati, Sergio, Attilio Agnoletto, and Maria Rosario Lazzati, eds. and trans. 1984. *La stregoneria. Diavoli, streghe, inquisitori dal Trecento al Settecento*. Milan: Mondadori.

Agrimi, Jole, and Chiara Crisciani. 1992. "Immagini e ruoli della 'vetula' tra sapere medico e antropologia religiosa (secoli XIII-XV)." In *Poteri carismatici e informali. Chiesa e società medievali*, eds. Agostino Paravicini Bagliani and André Vauchez, 224-61. Palermo: Sellerio.

Ankarloo, Bengt, and Stuart Clark, eds. 1999-2002. *The History of Witchcraft and Magic in Europe*. 6 vols. Philadelphia: University of Pennsylvania Press.

Bailey, Michael D. 2003. *Battling Demons: Witchcraft, Heresy, and Reform in the Late Middle Ages*. University Park (PA): Pennsylvania State University Press.

Barbierato, Federico. 2002. *Nella stanza dei circoli. Clavicula Salomonis e libri di magia a Venezia nei secoli XVII e XVIII*. Milan: Edizioni Sylvestre Bonnard.

Behringer, Wolfgang. 2004. *Witches and Witch-hunts: A Global History*. Cambridge (UK): Polity.

— 2006. "Malleus maleficarum." In *Encyclopedia of Witchcraft: The Western Tradition*, ed. Richard M. Golden, 3:717-23. Santa Barbara (CA): ABC-CLIO.

Benivieni, Antonio. 1994. *De Abditis Nonnullis ac Mirandis Morborum et Sanationum Causis*, ed. and trans. Giorgio Weber. Florence: Olschki.

Bertolin, Silvia, and Ezio Emerico Gerbore. 2003. *La stregoneria nella Valle d'Aosta medievale*. Aosta: Musumeci.

Bertolotti, Maurizio. 1991. "The Ox's Bones and the Ox's Hide: A Popular Myth, Part Hagiography and Part Witchcraft." In *Microhistory and the Lost Peoples of Europe: Selections from "Quaderni Storici,"* eds. Edward Muir and Guido Ruggiero, 42-70. Baltimore: Johns Hopkins University Press.

Bethencourt, Francisco. 1995. *L'Inquisition à l'époque moderne. Espagne, Portugal, Italie XVᵉ-XIXᵉ siècle*. Paris: Fayard.

Bever, Edward. 2006. "Molitor, Ulrich." In *Encyclopedia of Witchcraft: The Western Tradition*, ed. Richard M. Golden, 3:776-77. Santa Barbara (CA): ABC-CLIO.

Bianchi, alias de' Lancellotti, Tommasino. 1862-84. *Cronaca modenese*. 12 vols. Eds. Carlo Borghi, Luigi Lodi, and Giorgio Ferrari Moreni. Parma: Fiaccadori.

Biondi, Albano. 1977. "Streghe ed eretici nei domini estensi all'epoca dell'Ariosto." In *Il Rinascimento nelle corti padane. Società e cultura*, 165-99. Bari: De Donato.

— 1981. "La Signora delle erbe e la magia della vegetazione." In *Medicina erbe magia*, vol. 5 of *Cultura popolare nell'Emilia-Romagna*, 185-203. Milan: Silvana Editoriale.

— 1982. "Lunga durata e microarticolazione nel territorio di un Ufficio dell'Inquisizione. Il 'Sacro Tribunale' a Modena (1292-1785)." *Annali dell'Istituto storico italo-germanico in Trento*, VIII:73-90.

— 1989. "Introduzione" to *Libro detto Strega o delle illusioni del demonio*, by Giovanfrancesco Pico della Mirandola. Ed. Albano Biondi, trans. Leandro Alberti, 9-41. Venice: Marsilio.

Biondi, Grazia. 1993. *Benvenuta e l'Inquisitore. Un destino di donna nella Modena del '300*. Modena: Unione Donne Italiane - Centro documentazione donna.

Bonomo, Giuseppe. 1985. *Caccia alle streghe. La credenza nelle streghe dal sec. XIII al XIX con particolare riferimento all'Italia*, 3rd ed. Palermo: Palumbo.

Briggs, Robin. 1996. *Witches and Neighbors: The Social and Cultural Context of European Witchcraft*. New York: Viking.

Broedel, Hans Peter. 2003. *The Malleus Maleficarum and the Construction of Witchcraft: Theology and Popular Belief*. Manchester (UK)-New York: Manchester University Press.

Brucker, Gene, ed. 1971. *The Society of Renaissance Florence: A Documentary Study*. New York: Harper and Row.

Burke, Peter. 1977. "Witchcraft and Magic in Renaissance Italy: Gianfrancesco Pico and his *Strix*." In *The Damned Art: Essays in the Literature of Witchcraft*, ed. Sidney Anglo, 32-52. London: Routledge and K. Paul.

Cameron, Euan. 1992. "Italy." In *The Early Reformation in Europe*, ed. Andrew Pettegree, 188-214. Cambridge: Cambridge University Press.

Clark, Stuart. 1997. *Thinking with Demons: The Idea of Witchcraft in Early Modern Europe*. Oxford: Oxford University Press.

— 2002. "Witchcraft and Magic in Early Modern Culture." In *The Period of the Witch Trials*, eds. Bengt Ankarloo and Stuart Clark. Vol. 4 of *The History of Witchcraft and Magic in Europe*, eds. Bengt Ankarloo and Stuart Clark, 97-169. Philadelphia: University of Pennsylvania Press.

Cohen, Thomas, and Elizabeth Cohen. 1993. *Words and Deeds in Renaissance Rome: Trials Before the Papal Magistrates.* Toronto-Buffalo-London: University of Toronto Press.

Cohn, Norman. 1975. *Europe's Inner Demons: An Enquiry Inspired by the Great Witch-Hunt.* New York: Basic Books.

Coppo, Claudio, and Gian Maria Panizza. 1990. "La pace impossibile. Indagini e ipotesi per una ricerca sulle accuse di stregoneria a Triora." *Rivista di storia e letteratura religiosa*, XXVI:35-74.

Cross, Frank L., and E. A. Livingstone, eds. 1988. *Oxford Dictionary of the Christian Church*, 2nd ed. Oxford: Oxford University Press.

Dall'Olio, Guido. 2001. "Tribunali vescovili, Inquisizione romana e stregoneria. I processi bolognesi del 1559." In *Il piacere del testo. Saggi e studi per Albano Biondi*, ed. Adriano Prosperi, 63-82. Rome: Bulzoni.

Decker, Rainer. 2003. *Die Päpste und die Hexen: Aus den geheimen Akten der Inquisition.* Darmstadt: Primus.

Del Col, Andrea. 1988. "Organizzazione, composizione e giurisdizione dei tribunali dell'Inquisizione romana nella Repubblica di Venice (1500-1550)." *Critica storica*, XXV:244-94.

— 2000. "I criteri dello storico nell'uso delle fonti inquisitoriali moderne." In *L'Inquisizione romana. Metodologia delle fonti e storia istituzionale*, eds. Andrea Del Col and Giovanna Paolin, 51-72. Trieste: Edizioni Università di Trieste.

— 2006. *L'Inquisizione in Italia. Dal XII al XXI secolo.* Milan: Mondadori.

Delumeau, Jean. 1977. *Catholicism between Luther and Voltaire: A New View of the Counter-reformation.* London: Burns and Oates.

De Martino, Ernesto. 1966. *Sud e magia.* Milan: Feltrinelli.

Dinzelbacher, Peter. 2006. "Inquisition, medieval." In *Encyclopedia of Witchcraft: The Western Tradition*, ed. Richard M. Golden, 2:553-56. Santa Barbara (CA): ABC-CLIO.

Di Simplicio, Oscar. 2005. *Autunno della stregoneria. Maleficio e magia nell'Italia moderna.* Bologna: Il Mulino.

— 2006. "Italy." In *Encyclopedia of Witchcraft: The Western Tradition*, ed. Richard M. Golden, 2:574-79. Santa Barbara (CA): ABC-CLIO.

Duni, Matteo. 1999. *Tra religione e magia. Storia del prete modenese Guglielmo Campana (1460?-1541).* Florence: Olschki (Studi e testi per la storia religiosa del Cinquecento, 9).

— 2006a. "Alciati, Andrea." In *Encyclopedia of Witchcraft: The Western Tradition*, ed. Richard M. Golden, 1:29-30. Santa Barbara (CA): ABC-CLIO.

— 2006b. "Modena, Witchcraft Trials." In *Encyclopedia of Witchcraft: The Western Tradition*, ed. Richard M. Golden, 3:774-76. Santa Barbara (CA): ABC-CLIO.

— 2006c. "Skepticism." In *Encyclopedia of Witchcraft: The Western Tradition*, ed. Richard M. Golden, 4:1044-50. Santa Barbara (CA): ABC-CLIO.

Eamon, William. 1994. *Science and the Secrets of Nature: Books of Secrets in Medieval and Early Modern Culture*. Princeton: Princeton University Press.

Emison, Patricia. 1999. "Truth and *Bizzarria* in an Engraving of *Lo Stregozzo*." *The Art Bullettin*, LXXXI:623-36.

Ernst, Germana. 2006. "Cardano, Girolamo." In *Encyclopedia of Witchcraft: The Western Tradition*, ed. Richard M. Golden, 1:166-67. Santa Barbara (CA): ABC-CLIO.

Fantini, Maria Pia. 1996. "La circolazione clandestina dell'orazione di Santa Marta. Un episodio modenese." In *Donna, disciplina, creanza cristiana dal XV al XVII secolo. Studi e testi a stampa*, ed. Gabriella Zarri, 45-65. Rome: Edizioni di Storia e Letteratura.

— 1999. "Saggio per un catalogo bibliografico dai processi dell'Inquisizione. Orazioni, scongiuri, libri di segreti (Modena, 1571-1608)." *Annali dell'Istituto storico italo-germanico in Trento*, XXV:587-668.

Ferber, Sarah. 2004. *Possession and Exorcism in Early Modern France*. London-New York: Routledge.

Flint, Valerie I. J. 1991. *The Rise of Magic in Medieval Europe*. Oxford (UK): Clarendon Press.

Gentilcore, David. 1992. *From Bishop to Witch: The System of the Sacred in Early Modern Terra d'Otranto*. Manchester (UK)-New York: Manchester University Press.

— 1998. *Healers and Healing in Early Modern Italy*. Manchester (UK)-New York: Manchester University Press.

Ginzburg, Carlo. 1970. "Un letterato e una strega al principio del '500. Panfilo Sasso e Anastasia la Frappona." *Differenze* (Studi in memoria di Carlo Ascheri), IX:129-37.

— 1980. *The Cheese and the Worms: The Cosmos of a Sixteenth-century Miller*. Baltimore: The Johns Hopkins University Press.

— 1983. *The Night Battles: Witchcraft and Agrarian Cults in the Sixteenth and Seventeenth Century*. Baltimore-London: The Johns Hopkins University Press.

— and Marco Ferrari. 1986. "The Dovecote Has Opened Its Eyes: Popular Conspiracy in Seventeenth-century Italy." In *The Inquisition in Early Modern Europe: Studies on Sources and Methods*, eds. Gustav Henningsen and John Tedeschi, 190-98. DeKalb (IL): Northern Illinois University Press.

— 1989. "L'inquisitore come antropologo." In *Studi in onore di Armando Saitta dei suoi allievi pisani*, eds. Regina Pozzi and Adriano Prosperi, 23-33. Pisa: Giardini.

— 1990. "Witchcraft and Popular Piety: Notes on a Modenese Trial of 1519." In idem, *Myths, Emblems, Clues*, 1-16. London: Hutchinson Radius.

— 1991. *Ecstasies: Deciphering the Witches' Sabbath*. New York: Penguin.

Golden, Richard M., ed. 2006. *Encyclopedia of Witchcraft: The Western Tradition*. 4 vols. Santa Barbara (CA): ABC-CLIO.

Grottanelli, Cristiano. 1993. "Bambini e divinazione." In *Infanzie. Funzioni di un gruppo liminale dal mondo classico all'età moderna*, ed. Ottavia Niccoli, 23-72. Florence: Ponte alle Grazie.

Herzig, Tamar. 2006. "Witches, Saints, and Heretics: Heinrich Krämer's Ties with Italian Women Mystics." *Magic, Ritual, and Witchcraft*, I:24-55.

Housley, J. N. 1982. "Politics and Heresy in Italy: Anti-heretical Crusades, Orders and Confraternities." *Journal of Ecclesiastical History*, XXXIII:193-208.

Hsia, R. Po-chia. 2005. *The World of Catholic Renewal 1540-1770*, 2nd ed. Cambridge-New York: Cambridge University Press.

Kallestrup, Louise Nyholm. 2006. "Peña, Francisco." In *Encyclopedia of Witchcraft: The Western Tradition*, ed. Richard M. Golden, 3:888-89. Santa Barbara (CA): ABC-CLIO.

Kieckhefer, Richard. 1976. *European Witch Trials: Their Foundations in Popular and Learned Culture, 1300-1500*. London-Henley: Routledge and Kegan Paul.

— 1995. "The Office of the Inquisition and Medieval Heresy: The Transition from Personal to Institutional Jurisdiction." *Journal of Ecclesiastical History*, XLVI:36-61.

— 1998. *Forbidden Rites: A Necromancer's Manual of the Fifteenth*

Century. University Park (PA): Pennsylvania State University Press.

— 2000. *Magic in the Middle Ages*. Cambridge-New York: Cambridge University Press.

Kors, Alan Ch., and Edward Peters, eds. 2001. *Witchcraft in Europe 400-1700: A Documentary History*, 2nd ed. Philadelphia: University of Pennsylvania Press.

Kral, Giovanni. 1995. "Il viaggio di Zuan delle Piatte al Monte della Sibilla." In *Cultura d'élite e cultura popolare nell'arco alpino fra Cinque e Seicento*, eds. Ottavio Besomi and Carlo Caruso, 393-431. Basel-Boston-Berlin: Birkhäuser.

Krämer, Heinrich. 1971. *The Malleus Maleficarum of Heinrich Krämer and James Sprenger*, ed. and trans. Montague Summers. New York: Dover.

— 2007. *The Malleus Maleficarum*, ed. and trans. P. G. Maxwell-Stuart. Manchester (UK)-New York: Manchester University Press.

Lavenia, Vincenzo. 2001. "'Anticamente di misto foro.' Inquisizione, stati e delitti di stregoneria nella prima età moderna." In *Inquisizioni. Percorsi di ricerca*, ed. Giovanna Paolin, 35-80. Trieste: Edizioni Università di Trieste.

Lea, Henry Ch. 1957. *Materials Toward a History of Witchcraft*, ed. Arthur C. Howland, 3 vols. New York-London: Thomas Yoseloff.

Levack, Brian P. 2006. *The Witch-hunt in Early Modern Europe*, 3rd ed. London: Longman.

Liddell MacGregor Mathers, S., ed. and trans. 1889. *The Key of Solomon the King (Clavicula Salomonis)*. London: George Redway.

Macfarlane, Alan. 1970. *Witchcraft in Tudor and Stuart England: A Regional and Comparative Study*. London: Routledge and K. Paul.

Mammoli, Domenico, ed. 1972. *The Record of the Trial and Condemnation of a Witch, Matteuccia di Francesco, at Todi, 20 March 1428*. Rome: Cossidente.

Marcaccioli Castiglioni, Anna. 1999. *Streghe e roghi nel Ducato di Milano. Processi per stregoneria a Venegono Superiore nel 1520*. Milan: Thélema Edizioni.

Martin, Ruth. 1989. *Witchcraft and the Inquisition in Venice, 1550-1650*. Oxford: Blackwell.

Maxwell-Stuart, Peter G. 2006. "Spina, Alphonso de." In *Encyclopedia of Witchcraft: The Western Tradition*, ed. Richard M. Golden, 4:1080-81. Santa Barbara (CA): ABC-CLIO.

Monter, William, and John Tedeschi. 1986. "Toward a Statistical Profile of the Italian Inquisitions, Sixteenth to Eighteenth Centuries." In *The Inquisition in Early Modern Europe: Studies on Sources and Methods*, eds. Gustav Henningsen and John Tedeschi, 130-57. DeKalb (IL): Northern Illinois University Press.

— 2006. "Todi, Witch of." In *Encyclopedia of Witchcraft: The Western Tradition*, ed. Richard M. Golden, 4:1125-26. Santa Barbara (CA): ABC-CLIO.

Mormando, Franco. 1999. *The Preacher's Demons: Bernardino of Siena and the Social Underworld of Early Renaissance Italy*. Chicago: University of Chicago Press.

Muraro, Luisa. 1976. *La Signora del gioco. Episodi della caccia alle streghe*. Milan: Feltrinelli.

O'Neil, Mary R. 1984. "'Sacerdote ovvero Strione:' Ecclesiastical and Supersticious Remedies in 16th century Italy." In *Understanding Popular Culture: Europe from the Middle Ages to the Nineteenth Century*, ed. Steven L. Kaplan, 53-83. Berlin-New York-Amsterdam: Mouton.

— 1987. "Magical Healing, Love Magic and the Inquisition in Late Sixteenth-century Modena." In *Inquisition and Society in Early Modern Europe*, ed. Stephen Haliczer, 88-114. London-Sidney: Croom Helm,.

Ostorero, Martine, Agostino Paravicini Bagliani, Kathrin Utz Tremp, and Catherine Chène, eds. and trans. 1999. *L'imaginaire du sabbat. Édition critique des texts les plus anciens (1430 c.–1440 c.)*. Lausanne: Université de Lausanne.

Park, Katharine. 1985. *Doctors and Medicine in Renaissance Florence*. Princeton: Princeton University Press.

— 1998. "Medicine and Magic: The Healing Arts." In *Gender and Society in Renaissance Italy*, eds. Judith C. Brown and Robert C. Davis, 129-49. London-New York: Longman.

Peters, Edward. 1978. *The Magician, the Witch, and the Law*. Philadelphia: University of Pennsylvania Press.

— 1989. *Inquisition*. Berkeley-Los Angeles: University of California Press.

— 2002. "The Medieval Church and State on Superstition, Magic and

Witchcraft: From Augustine to the Sixteenth Century." In *The Middle Ages*, eds. Bengt Ankarloo and Stuart Clark. Vol. 2 of *The History of Witchcraft and Magic in Europe*, eds. Bengt Ankarloo and Stuart Clark, 173-245. Philadelphia: University of Pennsylvania Press.

Piccinini, Francesca, ed. 1997. *Civitas Geminiana. La città e il suo patrono*. Modena: Banco S. Geminiano e S. Prospero - Panini Editore.

Pico della Mirandola, Giovanfrancesco. 1989. *Libro detto Strega o delle illusioni del demonio*, ed. Albano Biondi, trans. Leandro Alberti. Venice: Marsilio.

— 2007. *La sorcière. Dialogue en trois livres sur la tromperie des démons*, ed. and trans. Alfredo Perifano. Turnhout: Brepols.

Prosperi, Adriano. 1996. *Tribunali della coscienza. Inquisitori, confessori, missionari*. Turin: Einaudi.

Rivera, Annamaria. 1988. *Il mago, il santo, la morte, la festa. Forme religiose nella cultura popolare*. Bari: Dedalo.

Romanello, Marina. 1975. "Un processo dell'Inquisizione a Modena." In *La stregoneria in Europa (1450-1650)*, ed. Marina Romanello, 119-31. Bologna: Il Mulino.

Romeo, Giovanni. 1990. *Inquisitori, esorcisti e streghe nell'Italia della Controriforma*. Florence: Sansoni.

— 2006. *L'Inquisizione nell'Italia moderna*, 3rd ed. Rome-Bari: Laterza.

Roper, Lyndal. 1994. *Oedipus and the Devil: Witchcraft, Sexuality and Religion in Early Modern Europe*. London-New York: Routledge.

— 2004. *Witch Craze: Terror and Fantasy in Baroque Germany*. New Haven-London: Yale University Press.

Ruggiero, Guido. 1993. *Binding Passions: Tales of Magic, Marriage, and Power at the End of the Renaissance*. New York–Oxford: Oxford University Press.

Russell, Jeffrey B. 1972. *Witchcraft in the Middle Ages*. Ithaca-London: Cornell University Press.

Schmitt, Jean-Claude. 2001. "Corps malade, corps possédé." In idem, *Le corps, les rites, les rêves, le temps. Essais d'anthropologie médiévale*, 319-43. Paris: Gallimard.

Siraisi, Nancy G. 1990. *Medieval and Early Renaissance Medicine: An Introduction to Knowledge and Practice*. Chicago-London: University of Chicago Press.

Stephens, Walter. 2002. *Demon Lovers: Witchcraft, Sex, and the Crisis of Belief*. Chicago-London: University of Chicago Press.

Tavuzzi, Michael. 1997. *Prierias: The Life and Works of Silvestro Mazzolini da Prierio, 1456-1527*. Durham (NC)-London: Duke University Press.

Tedeschi, John. 1990. "Inquisitorial Law and the Witch." In *Early Modern European Witchcraft: Centres and Peripheries*, eds. Bengt Ankarloo and Gustav Henningsen, 83-118. Oxford: Clarendon Press.

— 1991. *The Prosecution of Heresy: Collected Studies on the Inquisition in Early Modern Italy*. Binghamton (NY): Medieval and Renaissance Texts and Studies.

— 2000. *The Italian Reformation of the Sixteenth Century and the Diffusion of Renaissance Culture: A Bibliography of Secondary Literature*, in association with James M. Lattis. Modena: Panini.

Terpstra, Nicholas. 1996. "Confraternities and Mendicant Orders: The Dynamics of Lay and Clerical Brotherhood in Renaissance Bologna." *Catholic Historical Review*, LXXXII:1-22.

Thomas, Keith. 1971. *Religion and the Decline of Magic: Studies in Popular Beliefs in Sixteenth and Seventeenth Century England*. London: Weidenfeld and Nicholson.

Thorndike, Lynn. 1923-1958. *A History of Magic and Experimental Science*, 8 vols. New York: Columbia University Press.

Trenti, Giuseppe, ed. 2003. *I processi del tribunale dell'Inquisizione di Modena. Inventario generale analitico 1489-1784*. Modena: Aedes Muratoriana.

Valente, Michaela. 2006a. "Cassini, Samuele de." In *Encyclopedia of Witchcraft: The Western Tradition*, ed. Richard M. Golden, 1:172-73. Santa Barbara (CA): ABC-CLIO.

— 2006b. "Weyer, Johann." In *Encyclopedia of Witchcraft: The Western Tradition*, ed. Richard M. Golden, 4:1193-95. Santa Barbara (CA): ABC-CLIO.

Vanysacker, Dries. 2006. "Ponzinibio, Giovanni Francesco/ Gianfrancesco." In *Encyclopedia of Witchcraft: The Western Tradition*, ed. Richard M. Golden, 3:912-13. Santa Barbara (CA): ABC-CLIO.

Waite, Gary K. 2003. *Heresy, Magic, and Witchcraft in Early Modern Europe*. Houndsmill, Basingstoke (UK)-New York: Palgrave Macmillan.

Wiesner, Merry. 1993. *Women and Gender in Early Modern Europe*, Cambridge (UK)-New York: Cambridge University Press.

Zarri, Gabriella. 2006. "Spina, Bartolomeo della." In *Encyclopedia of Witchcraft: The Western Tradition*, ed. Richard M. Golden, 4:1081-82. Santa Barbara (CA): ABC-CLIO.

Illustrations

Fig. 1

Nicolò dell'Abate, *L'incontro dei triumviri* (detail). Fresco, 1546. Modena, Palazzo Comunale, Sala del Fuoco. Photo reproduced by permission of Museo Civico d'Arte, Modena.

Some of the most important buildings of Modena are recognizable in this view of the city, painted by one of the main protagonists of the Mannerist style in Emilia. The tallest building is the cathedral's bell-tower, known as the *Ghirlandina*, here represented without its characteristically tall steeple. To its left is the tower of the Town Hall (*Torre Civica*, or *Torre Mozza*), while to its right one sees the Clock Tower (*Torre dell'Orologio*).

Fig. 2

Unknown artist in *Bamberger Halsgerichtordnung*. Woodcut, 1508. Bamberg, Historisches Museum. Photo reproduced by permission of the Historisches Museum, Bamberg.

This woodcut depicts the strappado, the most common type of torture used by both secular and church courts—such as the Inquisition—in the late medieval and early modern period. The strappado (known in Italian as "la corda") consisted in tying the hands of the accused behind his or her back and to a pulley, with which the person would be lifted several feet above the ground. The judge could question the defendant thus suspended in the air, and order that the rope be jerked if confession was not forthcoming. This was a favored method because it enabled judges to choose the level of pain inflicted, keeping the defendant suspended above the ground as long as was deemed necessary, jerking the rope as often, and as hard, as they saw fit, depending on the prisoner's age, sex, and health. Weights (like the one seen in the foreground) could be tied to the ankles to heighten the pain of the defendant This woodcut also shows the officials of the court seated at a table, one of them in the process of writing down the trial's proceedings.

Fig. 3

Figs. 3-4-5-6
Unknown woodcut artist in Francesco Maria Guaccio, *Compendium Maleficarum*. Milan, Agostino Tradati, 1608. Photo reproduced by permission of the Biblioteca Civica Centrale of Torino.

Francesco Maria Guaccio's book, published at the beginning of the seventeenth century, is a conventional summary of witchcraft beliefs. However, it is unusual in that its written description of witches' nefarious deeds is systematically illustrated by woodcut images. We thus see male and female witches kissing the devil's buttocks as a sign of homage, then trampling on a wooden cross to seal their compact with the Enemy by defiling the most sacred Christian symbol (Fig. 4). The following woodcuts depict other atrocities traditionally ascribed to the witches, such as roasting and boiling infants (Fig. 5), or desecrating the dead to use body parts—especially those taken from the corpses of executed criminals—for deadly spells (Fig. 6).

Fig. 4
Unknown woodcut artist in Francesco Maria Guaccio, *Compendium Maleficarum*. Milan, Agostino Tradati, 1608. Photo reproduced by permission of the Biblioteca Civica Centrale of Torino.

Fig. 5
Unknown woodcut artist in Francesco Maria Guaccio, *Compendium Maleficarum*. Milan, Agostino Tradati, 1608. Photo reproduced by permission of the Biblioteca Civica Centrale of Torino.

Fig. 6
Unknown woodcut artist in Francesco Maria Guaccio, *Compendium Maleficarum*. Milan, Agostino Tradati, 1608. Photo reproduced by permission of the Biblioteca Civica Centrale of Torino.

Fig. 7

Figs. 7-8-9
Unknown woodcut artist in Ulrich Molitor, *De Lamiis et Pythonicis Mulieribus*. Reutlingen, Johann Othmar, 1489. Photo reproduced by permission of the Biblioteca Universitaria of Padova, courtesy of the Ministero per i Beni e le Attività Culturali.

The book *De Lamiis et Pythonicis Mulieribus* by the Swiss lawyer Ulrich Molitor was the first printed book on witchcraft to include pictures, and it rivalled the editorial success of the famous *Malleus Maleficarum*. The woodcuts reproduced here show three witches partly transformed into animals in the act of flying on a stick; two witches throwing a rooster and a snake into a cauldron to provoke a storm ("weather witches" were particularly feared in northern Europe); and a devil dressed as a man embracing a woman, likely a witch. The fame of this book owes so much to its illustrations that one tends to overlook the skeptical opinions of Molitor in regard to most of the depicted witches' feats.

165

Fig. 8
Unknown woodcut artist in Ulrich Molitor, *De Lamiis et Pythonicis Mulieribus*. Reutlingen, Johann Othmar, 1489. Photo reproduced by permission of the Biblioteca Universitaria of Padova, courtesy of the Ministero per i Beni e le Attività Culturali.

Fig. 9
Unknown woodcut artist in Ulrich Molitor, *De Lamiis et Pythonicis Mulieribus*. Reutlingen, Johann Othmar, 1489. Photo reproduced by permission of the Biblioteca Universitaria of Padova, courtesy of the Ministero per i Beni e le Attività Culturali.

Fig. 10

Fig. 10
Hans Baldung Grien, *Witches*. Chiaroscuro woodcut, 1510. London, The British Museum. Photo © The Trustees of the British Museum.

One of the most famous works by a well-known German artist who was fascinated by the theme of witchcraft, this woodcut represents a group of witches preparing for the ride to the sabbat in an inhospitable, solitary location. The sexual nature of witchcraft is suggested by the women's naked bodies, as well as by the powerful stream of vapors emerging from a jar held between the legs of the witch in the foreground, a clear sign that evil energy, capable of lifting a witch in the air (as seen in the upper left corner), originates from female genitalia. The human and animal skulls and bones shown in the lower left corner, the unsavory food (human flesh?) on the plate held by the old woman at the center, and above her, the two legs (of a baby?) sticking out of the vase carried by the witch who rides backwards on a goat, all hint at the deadly powers of witches and their deep enmity toward the human race.

Fig. 11

Fig. 11
Marcantonio Raimondi (attributed to), after Giulio Romano (?), *Lo Stregozzo* [*The Witches' Procession*]. Engraving, 1520s. Blanton Museum of Art, The University of Texas at Austin, The Leo Steinberg Collection, 2002 (photo: Rick Hall)

A powerful, disquieting work commonly thought to represent the procession to the witches' sabbat ("lo stregozzo", in sixteenth-century northern Italian vernacular), this masterful engraving is one of the most bewildering images of witchcraft produced in the Renaissance. In the upper right corner, it is easy to recognize the frightening figure of an old woman as that of a witch, shown in the act of crushing the head of an infant while other babies lie dead at her feet as she holds a flaming vase—two symbols of her deadly powers and her lustful nature. However, the function and meaning of the four muscular male nudes, the skeleton at the center of the picture, and the strange half-goat, half-bird creature, ridden by a fifth naked man, are far from clear. Most scholars interpret the engraving as a visual representation of the "Wild Hunt" as described by the Church canon *Episcopi*: the night ride of a motley throng composed of ghosts and monstrous creatures, led by a female deity often identified with the goddess Diana. It has recently been suggested that the work may refer to the famous 1523 witch-hunt of Mirandola—a town some twenty miles north-east of Modena in the lowlands between the rivers Secchia and Panaro. Given the likely date of the engraving, the background of its author, and the setting of the scene in a marshy terrain, this is an intriguing hypothesis (see Emison 1999).

Fig. 12

172

Fig. 12
Pedro Berruguete, *Auto-da-fé*. Oil on wood, circa 1500. Madrid, Museo del Prado. ©1995. Photo Scala, Firenze.

This work depicts an auto-da-fé, that is, the burning of several heretics (Cathars, in this case) at the hands of the Inquisition at the beginning of the thirteenth century. In the lower right corner of the painting two heretics are being burned at the stake (probably after having been strangled). Nearby, two others, wearing the garment and the pointed hat of the convicted heretic, are awaiting their turn while a Dominican friar is possibly trying to convert them at the last minute. Saint Dominic, the founder of the Dominican Order, is portrayed on a high tribune pardoning a fifth, hatless heretic who stands at the bottom of the stairway. Dominican friars were the backbone of the Inquisition in the majority of the Italian states. Although the painting refers to an earlier phase of the Inquisition's history, the same procedures and rituals would be followed for the auto-da-fé of convicted witches from the fifteenth century onwards.

Fig. 13

Fig. 13
Master of the Middle Rhine, *The Love Spell* (*Der Liebeszauber*) Tempera and oil on wood, mid fifteenth century. Leipzig, Museum der Bildenden Künste. Photo © Scala Firenze.

The painting, by an anonymous German artist, depicts a young enchantress in the act of casting a spell in a mood and a setting completely different from those of other contemporary representations of witchcraft. The slender figure of the naked woman, wearing only a pair of elegant slippers, stands at the center of a small but well-appointed room. Next to her, an open casket reveals a heart-shaped red object partly wrapped in the same thin silk veil which is gracefully draped over the woman's body. With her right hand she is squeezing a sponge, and holding with two fingers another dark object, perhaps a piece of charcoal from the room's fireplace. Drops of liquid fall from the sponge onto the heart, while the black object releases a stream of reddish spots that resemble sparks. The heart-shaped object is the clearest, though not the only, indication that the woman is casting a love spell, since her nudity, loose hair, and the simultaneous use of water and fire were well-known features of love magic techniques. The young man dressed in black—an appearance favored by the devil—seen peeping through the door is the only hint at the diabolical nature of the act, whereas the prevailing mood seems to be a self-satisfied enjoyment of the enchantress' beauty and of the elegant objects and furnishings of the room.

Fig. 14

Luca Signorelli, *The Damned* (detail). Fresco, 1499-1503. Orvieto cathedral, Chapel of San Brizio (Cappella Nuova). Photo ©Scala Firenze.

This detail from Signorelli's fresco masterpiece has long been thought to depict a devil carrying a sinful woman to her eternal punishment in Hell. Recent studies, however, point to the sexual intimacy suggested by the two figures' interlaced fingers, and propose that the woman might represent a witch who had a liaison with a demon during her lifetime (see Stephens 2002).

Fig. 15

Master of San Geminiano, *Stories of Saint Geminiano* (detail). Limestone relief, circa 1106-1110. Modena cathedral, architrave of the Porta dei Principi. Provided by Archivio Fotografico del Museo Civico d'Arte, Modena.

This work by an aid of Wiligelmo—the great master of Romanesque sculpture—represents one of the most celebrated miracles of Geminiano, bishop of Modena in the fourth century and eventually the city's patron saint. According to tradition, Geminiano had exorcized the daughter of the Roman Emperor Jovianus, expelling the demon that possessed her body. The saint is shown on the left of the relief holding the girl's hand and successfully driving out the demon, who departs in the shape of a monstrous owl. Geminiano's great fame as an exorcist made the crypt of the cathedral of Modena, where he was buried, one of the choice locations in northern Italy for the exorcism of the possessed.

Fig. 16

Fig. 16

Agostino di Duccio, *Stories of Saint Geminiano* (detail). Marble relief, 1442. Modena cathedral, south side. Photo reproduced by permission of the Museo Civico d'Arte, Modena.

This scene, carved in a characteristic Renaissance style, is part of a monumental bas-relief frieze which originally decorated the altar of Saint Geminiano, revered as the most sacred in the cathedral of Modena since it stands over the saint's tomb in the crypt. The Florentine sculptor Agostino di Duccio portrays Geminiano wearing his bishop's mitre while exorcizing the emperor's daughter.

Index

INDEX

184

gist, 16
Jesus Christ, 16, 52, 68-69, 87-88, 90, 106, 108, 115, 117-18
John XXII, pope, 27
Jovianus, Roman emperor, 177
Krämer, Heinrich, inquisitor and demonologist, 18-19
Lady of the Game (Domina ludi), 43
Lady of the Course (Domina cursus), 43-44
La Menigotta, accused witch, see "Menigotta"
Lecco, 35
Liber Centum Regum, magic handbook, 47
Liber Iuratus, magic handbook, 47
Lombardy, 7, 18, 22, 29-31
Lucifer, see Satan
Machiavelli, Pietro Gian Paolo, 56
Madonna Oriente, 28
Magnanini, Geminiano, priest, 90
Malleus Maleficarum (Krämer), 18-19, 30, 36, 43-44, 49, 165
Mamoris, Pierre, demonologist, 16
Mangialoca, Benvenuta, see "Benincasa, Benvenuta"
Mangialoca, Manfredino, accused wizard, 47
Mantovani, Eleonora, 99-100
Mantovani, Giovanna, 99-100
Maranello, 68, 73, 113-15, 117
Marco, Servite friar, 81
Marescotti, Bernardino, 89-90, 93
Maria, niece of Eleonora Mantovani, 99
Marianus Teutonic, physician, 114
Maroverti, Caterina, 65
Mary, the Virgin, 68-69, 87, 115, 118, 120-21, 123
Mascarelli, Gaspare, husband of Giovanna, 60, 82-83
Mascarelli, Giovanna, 60, 82-83
Master of San Geminiano, sculptor, 177
Master of the Middle Rhine, painter, 175
Matteo of Monfestino, priest, 120
Matteuccia di Francesco, accused witch, 29
Medici, Lorenzo de', 20
Menigotta, la, accused witch, 63-64
Merlo, Pietro, weeder, 86
Mesola, 122
Mezardi, Marchione, 80
Michele Antonio, father of Andriola, see Andriola
Milan, 7, 28, 31, 34, 43
Mirandola, 31, 171
Moceno, Simone, accused wizard, 104
Mocogno, 122
Modena, 7, 8, 28, 31-34, 42-75, 80-125, 159, 177-79

Churches
San Domenico, 44, 91
San Geminiano, cathedral, 65-66, 104, 107, 123, 177-79
San Giorgio, 80
San Girolamo, 85
San Lazzaro, 82, 84
San Michele, 47, 51, 82, 85, 90, 92
Neighborhoods
San Bartolomeo, 80-1
San Pietro, 80
Molinari, Caterina, 103
Molitor, Ulrich, lawyer and demonologist, 21, 165-67
Montagnana, Antonio, priest, lover of Bernardina Stadera, 48, 80-81, 90, 93
Montanari, Scontra, 116
Montano, Sebastiano, priest, 54
Montecuccoli, Ercole, vicar of Modena's inquisitor, 118-19, 124
Morano, Bianca, 56
Morano, Giovanni Niccolò, 98
Nider, Johannes, demonologist, 16, 20
Nonantola, 73, 110, 112
Orsolina, nicknamed la Rossa, see "Toni, Orsolina"
Ottaviano of Castel Bolognese, suffragan bishop of Ferrara, 119, 124
Padela, la, accused witch, 43
Palli, Giovanna, accused witch, 43, 45
Panaro River, 171
Pantaleario, evil spirit, 103, 106
Papacy, also: the Holy See, 7-8, 17-19, 23, 27, 32-35, 61, 104, 107
Paris, University of, 12, 59
Parma, 31, 86
Pasini, Antonio, husband of Lucrezia, 85
Pasini, Lucrezia, nicknamed Gotola, 65-66, 85-86, 93
Paul III, pope, 32
Paul IV, pope, 33
Pazzani, Margherita, 62-65
Pelloni, Gaspare, 80-81
Pelloni, Jacopo, priest, 80-81
Peña, Francisco, jurist, 36
Perugia, 29
Picatrix, magic handbook, 46-47
Pico della Mirandola, Gianfrancesco, philosopher, 31
Pico della Mirandola, Giovanni, philosopher, 31
Piedmont, 18
Pietro d'Arezzo, accused wizard, 57
Pinelli, Niccolò, 115
Pius V, pope, 33